Date Due

AN EXPERIMENT IN FRIENDSHIP

By David Hinshaw

THE HOME FRONT

A MAN FROM KANSAS

AN EXPERIMENT IN FRIENDSHIP

AN EXPERIMENT IN
Friendship

By DAVID HINSHAW

G. P. PUTNAM'S SONS
New York

My trip to Finland in the summer of 1946 to inspect the work of the American Friends Service Committee and note the Committee's and Finland's needs and gather data for this book was done without cost to the Service Committee. The preparation of the book also has been a labor of love. The publishers, G. P. Putnam's Sons, are contributing all profits from the book's sale to the Finland division of the Service Committee.

DAVID HINSHAW

January, 1947
Dunmow Farm
West Chester
Pennsylvania

CONTENTS

Sixteen pages of photographic illustrations follow page 68.

INTRODUCTION

By Rufus M. Jones

EVERY GENERATION has its list of heroes, the stuff out of which epics are made. Unfortunately Homers do not come very often to create the epic. This book will reveal to the reader that the heroes are very much in evidence, and though David Hinshaw had no thought of creating an epic, his plain, unadorned, straightforward story, of what he has seen with his eyes and heard with his ears and his hands have handled, gives his story, in spite of himself, an epic quality. He went out to see, with no thought of making a book, but the moving events, the thrilling experiences, the heroic work, which came before his eyes caused this book to walk right off his writing pad and confront the reader with its vivid objectivity and reality.

The Quakers who are behind this work of human relief are not in the proper sense of the word a "sect." They do not focus upon creeds or religious forms, and they have no order of priests. They constitute rather a spiritual *movement,* the members of which aim to have direct firsthand experience of God operating in and through the life of man, giving inward certainty and marching power, and out of this experience has come to these Quakers a passion for human service, an eagerness to take up and to share the burden of the world's suffering. They have been in almost every country where there is serious trouble. They have not only fed the hungry, clothed the naked, and built homes for the homeless, but what is even more important, they have entered into living sympathy with those that have suffered, and they have made the reality of divine love a little more real by the fact of the human love that flowed out spontaneously through them. This Quaker passion for human service is not a late arrival in the Quaker movement. It was born with the birth of the movement itself. It was the very elemental stuff of the spirit of George Fox, the founder. It has burst forth in a unique way in a succession of notable persons through the three hundred years of Quaker history—John Bellers, John Woolman, Elizabeth Fry, William Allen, Joseph Sturge, Lucretia Mott, John G. Whittier, down to the men and women of today.

It was Joseph Sturge who after the Crimean War of 1854 took up the task of extensive relief in this same Finland, trying in some small degree to repair the damage which the British fleet had inflicted on the Bothnian peasants in the shelling of their towns. Whittier in his memorial poem on Joseph Sturge, describing the sorrow that came from many lands at the news of his death, says that it came

> From the locked roadsteads of the Bothnian peasants,
>   And harbors of the Finn,
> Where war's worn victims saw his gentle presence
> Come sailing, Christ-like, in,

> To seek the lost, to build the old waste places,
>   To link the hostile shores
> Of severing seas, and sow with England's daisies
> The moss of Finland's moors.

But Quakers in the last century did not have the technique of the work camp, which is so admirably described in Chapter VIII of this book, and which is a strikingly effective method of purveying both material help and that more subtle form of assistance which we call spiritual fortification. This latest band of Quakers who have gone out to help Finland in its time of need have not sown the moss of its moors with American daisies, but they have planted seeds of love in the hearts of its people, and the children of the land will never forget the love that has come to them.

AN EXPERIMENT IN FRIENDSHIP

CHAPTER I

The Story behind the Story

THE TIME: After supper on a midsummer day in 1946. The sun is still high in the sky, for there is daylight around the clock at this season of the year.

The place: Rovaniemi, Finland, just under the Arctic Circle, the capital city of the Lapland province, nine out of ten of whose buildings had been war-destroyed two years earlier.

The setting: A one-story wooden barracks surrounded by gaunt chimneys and heaps upon heaps of rubble which once had been homes. The stark chimneys, pointing their bony fingers to the sky, seem to be sentinels warning mankind of the waste, horror, and futility of war. Here and there homes and business buildings in different stages of construction are seen rising from the surrounding rubble.

The sound of hammer striking nail is heard as men and women, hard driven by the inevitable coming of the cold, hurry the hammer harder and faster. One-horse carts and charcoal-powered trucks rumble along the streets carrying building materials and their large cans or barrels of water. The town has no water system, hence all water must be hauled from wells or the near-by river. Children's voices rise and fall on all sides as they play games in the piles of bricks and stones which once had been homes.

Inside the barracks in one of its four rooms, three Americans, two women and a man, dressed much as they would be in the States, are washing and drying dishes, carrying in water which is to be boiled on a wood-burning kitchen stove for the next day's drinking. The presence in the community of several cases of paratyphoid makes this and other precautions necessary.

The telephone rings—for the kitchen-dining-living room serves also as an office. One of the women answers it but soon calls for help because she is unable to understand everything the troubled Finn tries to tell her. The interpreter, a young Finnish helper, learns that a sick child is being hurried in a truck to the barracks from a village fifty miles away and that the parents want the "Quekars" (as the Finns call them) to look after the child.

The three members of the Quaker field staff quickly make their plans. They telephone a doctor and make certain that he will be able to come at call; they prepare a cot for the child. These things done, they go on with the conversation and housework as though there had been no interruption. They talk of friends and home so far away and of their work, but mostly they talk about their good friends, the wholly admirable Finns.

These three, the two women, both college graduates, and the man, a professor of philosophy in an American college, on leave of absence, are in Finland with two other compatriots to direct the Quaker program of helping feed and clothe the people of war-ravaged Finland and to perform for them a great variety of other helpful services all of which were made possible by the contributions of Finnish-Americans.

The request over the telephone to look after the sick child, though not in line with their main purpose, is not an unusual interruption of routine, because the Finns, after eight months, have come to believe that the resourceful Quakers can and will handle any emergency.

It is ten o'clock by the time they have completed housekeeping and finished making arrangements to care for the child. Since he should arrive within an hour or so there is no point in going to bed, so they adjourn to the steps outside the barracks to join in singing Finnish and American songs with the young Finnish and Swedish women from the adjoining barracks who look after the children of the day nursery. When the sick child arrives, they care for him and comfort and calm his anxious parents; the doctor arrives to diagnose the case; midnight and all's well.

Every hour of their day, which had begun at seven o'clock that morning, had been filled with a great variety of kindly services. Food had been hurried off in trucks to many different schools, each school getting the amount and kind it required. Nails from Sweden for home reconstruction were urgently needed, and efforts had been made to speed their delivery. A health nurse had reported a sick and impoverished family some miles away, and their more pressing needs had been provided.

No one could anticipate what kind of request for help the frequently ringing telephone would bring, who the next caller would be, or what his needs. The frequency and variety of requests on the face of it should create confusion and dissipate effort. But to the observer's astonishment neither confusion nor lost motion evidenced themselves, whereas calmness and efficiency were the rule at all times. Each request, though unrelated to the previous one, seemed to fit in naturally with the pattern of their efforts; all of them together spelled human service, performed with warm, generous responsiveness and the same willingness with which one friend tries to help another.

A Finnish schoolboy wrote the Quaker staff:

The "Quekars" have conquered the hearts of all children with their radiant and joyous essences [personalities]. I cannot find the words for how grateful I am but I will wish God's blessings to "Quekars", to America, Ya, to all these men and women who have remembered us, the children of poor Finland.

Another boy, in the fourth grade, addressed them as "My best friends, the 'Quekars.'" He told of the arrival of the first food allotment and the excitement of his companions while carrying it into the schoolhouse. "Now we have eaten many good meals," he said and added ecstatically, "It has been as if I could go up to the sky."

Go anywhere in Lapland and ask a resident for directions to a "Quekar" project, and then watch his tired, trouble-seamed face lighten, his eyes brighten as he gives you exact and detailed directions.

These expressions of their attitude toward the efforts of the staff to help them in their tragic and terrible emergency reflect with reasonable accuracy how the Finns appraise what has been done to help them help themselves, to heal the scars of war, and to "build bridges of friendship which nothing will ever destroy.

Mother will tell daughter about it, father will tell son, during the coming years."

I visited the Quaker relief projects in the Lapland province of Finland in July 1946, and later went to central and southern Finland where Friends will concentrate their major activities during the 1946–47 season and undertake to be of useful service to all those in greatest need, among whom are the 420,000 tragic evacuees from the former Finnish province of Karelia ceded by the 1944 peace treaty to Russia.

Everywhere I conferred with local and national government and social welfare officials and other leaders about the present and future relief program. The unity of their purpose and method was inspiring. I left tragic Finland with a heavy heart, lightened only by the magnificent courage and the vast industry of a people whose hope is so inspiring and challenging that it renews faith in God and man.

The Lapland program had reached its maximum when I arrived there. It included one or more supplemental meals daily to more than 23,000 children in 270 schools, orphanages, nurseries, and homes. With the aid of the Finnish Red Cross and local committees the staff had distributed 173 tons of clothing and shoes and 117 tons of supplies other than food. It was also operating two work camps and helping in the conduct of a third; in these, seventy-seven volunteers were building or repairing homes and performing many other helpful services without cost to the inhabitants.

This book is primarily a case study of their program in Finland, and as such, it presents and interprets the broad pattern and purpose of Quaker humanitarian work in other countries. It seeks to make available an explanation not only of what they try to do but how and why they do it.

Today the Quakers, with a world membership of approximately 140,000 (about 118,000 in the United States, 20,000 in England, 200 in France and Germany each, 172 in Sweden—the remainder scattered in a half-dozen or more other countries), are conducting experiments in friendship in the United States and the following twelve foreign countries: Austria, China, Finland, France, Germany, Hungary, India, Italy, Japan, Mexico, Norway, and Poland.

The Service Committee's budget for work in these thirteen countries for the calendar year of 1947 is $8,365,326. This does not include gifts in kind which are estimated to reach $1,500,000 in value. Non-Quakers provide the Committee with approximately 85 per cent of its funds. Quaker contributions cover not only all administration costs, which in 1946 were $309,800, but in addition they supply at least ten cents to each non-Quaker-contributed dollar which is expended for direct relief. Each non-Quaker dollar given to the Service Committee thus performs one dollar and ten cents' worth of humanitarian service.

The Committee's field activities are directed by a staff of two hundred carefully selected and trained volunteer workers, about one third of whom are Quakers. These field workers are assisted in their tasks by an estimated minimum of 20,000 volunteers who live in the areas served. Thus the services of each Quaker field worker are magnified three hundred times by those of non-Quaker volunteer workers.

Quaker consciences are troubled because the general public is prone to give them sole credit for the Service Committee's work. They try constantly to correct this misapprehension by giving full credit to the indispensable co-operation of non-Quaker workers and contributors. This book will establish clearly that Quakers serve mainly as the spiritual leaven in the loaf which expresses the helpful purpose of men and women of good will of every religious group and every nationality.

So far, the Quakers have enjoyed the friendly co-operation of public officials and of every group, American or foreign, engaged in work which ran parallel with any of their own undertakings—in the end, that is. In a few interesting cases unanimous support has been lacking at the time of launching a project. But before the job was finished their performance always has won the approval of their associates. Failure in this would convince them that they themselves had failed.

One high church official in Finland, for example, in 1945, was unenthusiastic about the Quaker plans for service in Finland. He seemed to fear that the Quakers would use their work to increase their membership in his country although there were only nine Quakers in all Finland. One year after the Service Committee's program was started, this same official remarked, "I greatly admire the Quakers and I hope in time to qualify for a third-class membership in the Society of Friends."

In Italy, where Quaker workers are making 7,000 rooms habitable each month in 150 destroyed villages, some church officials at first were a bit suspicious of their motives. Later the same officials, after careful investigation, reported, "The Quakers are good people. Their only desire is to help those in need."

In India the Quaker program now has the complete co-operation of every important individual, official and group, from Gandhi to Wavell, including the Moslem League.

The answer to the question of how it happens that the Quakers perform such services is found in the fact that three hundred years ago, when the movement was started, unrelenting persecution made its membership a compact body. Interpreting literally the scriptural command "Return good for evil," they brought works to their faith.

George Fox, founder of the Quaker movement, reports in one place in his journal:

> . . . when they (the justices and captains) understood the business Friends met about, and saw their books and accounts of collections for relief of the poor, how we took care one county to help another, and to help our Friends beyond the seas, and provide for our poor that none of them should be chargeable to their parishes, etc., the justices and officers confessed we did their work, and passed away peaceably and lovingly, commending Friends' practices.

The pioneer social workers of their time and clime, they drew a pattern for humanitarian service which they have changed but little during the generations. In Finland, as elsewhere, these modern Quakers reduce their problems to terms of common understanding, buckle on "the armor of the spirit," and work with hands made tenderly skillful by service for the glory of the God of all men—never for the glory of their movement or its beliefs. They attempt, in spite of obvious human faults and failings, to transform dollars into spiritual instruments through living testimony to their conviction that love is the strongest power for good in the world.

A unique feature of their humanitarian work is that when they seek out distressed areas for service, they prefer those which, for whatever reason, other humanitarian organizations avoid or neglect. In such places they extend the hand of sincere friendship to men of all creeds, color, and nationalities. In their effort to bring divine law and human law together, they busy themselves with the simple work of binding wounds and of satisfying physical and spiritual hunger. By such means they often are able to help desperate, struggling people through difficult situations and tragic periods.

Almost equally important is the fact that their humanitarian service gives hope and encouragement for a better society to large numbers of men and women of good will. During the war years, for example, Clarence E. Pickett, who has so ably and understandingly directed the work of the Service Committee during the past fifteen momentously troubled years, expressed the belief in a general letter that the primary obligation of the Committee may soon be "to speak for those who will be hated and neglected: Finland, defeated and ruined, chaotic Poland, and the spiritually broken people of Germany."

This letter was read by a United States soldier serving in the Philippines. He replied: "I read your words and the sentiments of your organization with the most heart-warming gratitude. That fine spirit in a world seething with hate and vindictiveness is indeed encouraging. In the hearts of those who believe and practice forgiveness, charity and kindness burn the few lights of a blacked-out world. . . ."

The Quakers would be less than human if they were not deeply touched by the fact that the nature of their service and methods of giving it inspires the respect of members of other religious denominations, each of whom "puts his own religious denomination first, although many, on mature reflection, would give second place to the Society of Friends." This favorable ranking brings the Society few members, but it does help increase their opportunities for useful, human service. And to them that is the important thing, because they seek with neighborly kindness to quicken the hearts of all men with whom they come in contact. They neither want nor seek anything for themselves. They nurture only the hope that through such service they will be able to create oases of friendship all over the world which in time may become bases for universal peace.

Absurd? Perhaps! But to them their purpose and efforts do not seem absurd. They believe with simple faith that some group must ever hold high before the eyes of men the bright goal of a peaceable, kindly world. Realists undoubtedly hold their way to be ineffective. That the realists may be right does not weaken Quaker faith in the eternal rightness of following the urge of their hearts and consciences.

Reasoning aside, who knows whence a homing pigeon's instinct comes?

Some readers may get the impression from these pages that Quakers, individually and collectively, are almost too good for this world. This is far from true. Some Quakers have been accurately characterized as "spiritual snobs," "cantankerous," or "opinionated." A majority of the members of the Society shares the average number of human faults and weaknesses. But their reputation as a group indicates that these proponents of good will have cultivated with considerable success some of the human virtues.

The saving grace of their religious movement is that the way of life and form of worship of its members is capable of producing an exceptional number of saintly characters who by precept and example exert a powerful influence on the life and works of its followers. Their influence is made particularly manifest in the group's social welfare work. Throughout three centuries this service has remained their real claim to spiritual fame. In it are strikingly realized their ideals of tolerance, kindness, integrity, and helpfulness. And in it can most readily be discerned the guidance of an "Inner Light."

The purpose of this book is not, however, to argue the Quakers' case nor to make saints or sinners out of them. It is to describe one of their many relief projects. It is conceivable that in doing so it might lose the Service Committee a little financial support because it strips their work of the magic which, many non-Quakers seem to believe, surrounds it. This factual story shows clearly that there is no magic in the methods of their humanitarian service. They are as direct as the questions of a child; as simple as two plus two, as naïve as truth, as impartial as rain; their guiding principles as old as the morning star—and yet as young.

CHAPTER II

Finland and the Finns

AFTER THE Russian Communist revolution in 1917 Finland declared her independence through her legally elected Diet. Her new independent status was recognized almost immediately by several states: France, Soviet Russia, Germany, and the Scandinavian countries, and later the United States and the United Kingdom. Finland was one of the first countries to recognize Soviet Russia, and the peace treaty of Tartu (Dorpat, 1920) confirmed the political frontiers, which enclosed no ethnical minorities. Finland took nothing from anybody, and her independence and international status threatened nobody.

A tragic civil war in 1918, between leftist workers allied with Russian Red guards who had been slow to return to Russia and a rightist army aided by German soldiers and equipment, was fought out. The rightists were victorious. The Allied victory over the German armies soon brought to an end all German support and influence. Soon a wise and moderate political freedom was established that helped restore unity and opened the way for Finland's era of progress.

Independent Finland adopted immediately a constitution which corresponded to her democratic traditions. It is similar in many ways to the American constitution; the president is chosen by special electors for a term of six years, the parliament is elected by the people on a basis of equal and unrestricted franchise—Finland was the first country in Europe to grant the vote to women. As in our own constitution, the fundamental civic rights were granted and guarded: freedom of speech and assembly, freedom of faith, freedom of the press.

So began the golden age of Finland. Her record of social, economic, and political progress between 1917 and 1937 is unparalleled in the history of civilization. This amazing feat was accomplished despite the fact that only one acre out of every ten in all Finland is suitable for either farming or pasturage. Three quarters of her total area is given over to forest; the rest is wasteland or water.

The statistics in the appendix are necessary as aids to realization of the social and economic transformation in Finland. Her fabulous economic advance was carried out with balanced budgets. She met her foreign obligations in full the day they were due; she invested huge sums, for such a small country, in agricultural and industrial equipment; and she pulled her standards of living up by her own bootstraps, so to speak. She weathered the world depression of the nineteen-thirties and went forward shaken but sure.

The racial background on which these achievements have been built is largely northern European. The old idea that Finns are of Mongolian extraction is now without support. The prevailing characteristics of the people are those of the fair races, including fair hair and blue or gray eyes. Actual settlement of Finland began in the

Iron Age, about the first century A.D., by an influx of Magyar immigrants from the Volga basin, whose language was somewhat similar to that of the Hungarians, wholly unlike Russian or German. The few Lapps who inhabited Finland at that time slowly retreated northward. Ancient skeletons indicate that the Lapps, who now inhabit the northern edges of Norway, Sweden, Finland, and Russia, were akin to the Mongolians. But in Finland, at least, long proximity has blended Finnish blood with that of their southern compatriots.

Throughout the centuries the Finns have preserved and developed their democratic processes. My arrival in Finland, by chance, was timed perfectly to see a practical demonstration of how the Finns make democracy work. Governor Hannula of the Lapland province invited me to attend a conference and dinner on the evening of my first day in Rovaniemi.

This gathering was part of an all-day conference which he, with some members of the cabinet from Helsinki, was holding with citizens of the community.

An English-speaking Finn interpreted for me in an undertone what the speakers had to say. Each of the local citizens was given an opportunity to speak. The point each made was explained or answered by the official in whose department it came.

A postmaster sharply criticized the government's failure to push completion of the post office. He expressed the opinion that it was more important to provide adequate space for the mails than to concentrate on highway and railroad repairs.

The minister of communications in reply explained that Finland's life and commerce depended directly upon the ability of her people to transport food and goods; that without open highways and operating railroads each community would have to live off its own resources. He then detailed the exact status of highway repairs and gave a time schedule for the completion of this work.

One by one each man there got his troubles off his chest or offered his suggestions for the help of others. As is the case with men everywhere, each speaker dwelt upon his own particular needs or interests. But when the meeting ended, it seemed impossible, to an outsider, for anyone present to leave without having been helped to see that everything was being done, and well done, for the good of the nation as a whole.

In the field of foreign policy the Finnish Republic had from the beginning only one aim: to live in peace and peaceful co-operation with other countries, maintaining her position as a free people among other free nations. She took an active part in the efforts of the League of Nations to build up a lasting peace and joined with the Scandinavian countries in their policy of strict neutrality. She based her relations with Russia upon the peace treaty of 1920. To this was added in 1932 a treaty of nonaggression which, by a later extension, was to be binding until 1945.

In line with her wish to remain neutral, Finland never joined any group of big powers. The majority of her citizens tried always instead to stand aside from their conflicts. It was this policy which in the spring of 1939 led her to reject an offer from Hitler to conclude a nonaggression pact with the Reich; and she did so at the risk of incurring Germany's dangerous resentment. Her immediate motive was her desire to emphasize her complete freedom from every entanglement with Nazi Germany.

Finland's firm purpose to follow the line of neutrality

was clear and generally recognized. Thus Mr. Joseph E. Davies, the U.S. ambassador to Moscow, after a close study of the Finnish question, wrote to his government in a report dated August 2, 1939:

The net impression which I get (and it is quite strong) from these various conversations is that the government of Finland is innately hostile to the Hitler concept and his governmental policies. Finland is instinctively not pro-German.... Finland's policy is based upon a realization of the exceedingly precarious geographical and military strategic position she occupies between two powerful enemy countries, and upon a determination realistically to avoid antagonizing either, if possible, and in any event to do her utmost to prevent her from being converted into a battle-ground, whereby both her political independence and economic freedom and independent well-being might be destroyed.

For the reasons given by Ambassador Davies, it has been Finland's fate to be enmeshed in wars, for all of the eagerness of her people to avoid them. In 1939 when Nazi Germany's aggressive moves startled the world and convinced Russia of the necessity of taking protective countermeasures, which included plans to fortify and control certain points in Finland considered highly strategic, the Finnish government demurred, and in consequence found herself at war with a neighbor too powerful to resist for long. Accordingly, in March 1940, she signed a treaty of peace with Moscow, yielding to Russia's demands. Several other small states in Europe, believing that interests of safety counseled joining the Axis at this time, did not hesitate to do so. The government of Finland, however, continued to hold out. Its determination to maintain Finnish neutrality in spite of everything had the earnest and undivided support of the Finnish people.

In June 1941 Hitler tore up the German-Russian agreement of August 1939 and invaded the Soviet Union. Under pressure from Germany, Finland found herself again at war with Russia. She fought, however, neither for the German Reich nor for its war aims, although she did permit Germany to establish military bases in Lapland from which the Nazis attacked Allied convoys to Murmansk and supported their military operations in northern Norway. Actually, however, Finland was fighting her own separate war in a desperate effort to preserve her independence and democratic liberty and to keep the poor Finnish soil in her own hands.

Finland made peace with Russia in the summer of 1944. The terms provided that Finland would (1) pay Russia $300,000,000 over a brief period of years—two payments have been made to date; the balance is due in six additional annual payments; (2) cede to Russia slightly more than 10 per cent of her territory; (3) drive the Nazi troops out of Lapland. She drove the Nazis out; she ceded the territory to Russia; and she is making reparation payments as they become due, despite the great strain they make on her economy and standard of living.

One of Finland's first major problems is to find food enough for her people, her most precious asset. Next, she must provide shelter for them. This latter need was especially pressing in Lapland, where the "scorched earth" destruction program carried out by a regiment of Storm Troopers imported for the purpose was frightful. Two years later there were evidences everywhere of this sweeping and thorough destruction. Hillsides were covered with blackened ruins of what once were homes (the basic units of society, which nurture and protect the bodies, the minds, hearts, and aspirations of every individual in all the world). Many of the holocaust's survivors nurtured their bodies, minds, and hearts in earthen-floored cellars. In them families of five or more children and their parents lived, ate, and slept. Others, sometimes thirty or more people of all ages, lived in unpainted, furnitureless barracks. A few had finished rebuilding their homes. Pointing to a bookcase, one woman said: "This was the only thing I was able to save from my home." Bridges were destroyed, railroad tracks twisted. And where a church once had stood was marked a great X on civilization. Government planes were stationed all over Finnish Lapland, ready at an instant's notice to hurry to a hospital with another man, woman, or child who had been injured by a hidden mine. A man who had seen it the day before described to me the killing of a herd of two hundred reindeer in a mine field.

In one town, Rovaniemi, the capital city of the north, which is in the same degree of latitude as Nome, Alaska, the Nazi troops destroyed 850 homes and buildings, or 87 per cent of all structures in the town; they destroyed 90 per cent of Enontekio and almost 100 per cent of Kittila. In the latter place they left a few sheds and a great Lutheran church which stands at the edge of town, back of whose cemetery I counted ninety-two white crosses marking the graves of Kittila's soldier dead. The community had a prewar population of fifteen hundred. No one knows why the Nazis spared Kittila's Lutheran church. Speculation has it that the Storm Trooper in charge may have been a member of that faith. On the other hand the hot pursuit of the Finnish troops may have hurried the Nazis out of town before they could get around to the church. Whatever the reason for its being spared, it proved a blessing to the former residents who returned to Kittila in the fall of 1945, the church serving as a dormitory for all of them—a dry, warm place where they could sleep and eat and exist.

Thus in Lapland also the Finnish government and people must do more than merely provide food and clothing to sustain life and protect bodies. They must also rebuild homes, factories, and business buildings, and repair or replace their transportation system.

THE FINNS

Few people ever have more greatly needed both material and spiritual aid than did the Finns when the Quaker workers reached Lapland in late 1945. In telling of their arrival, one of the staff reported: "Conditions are terrible, but the people are wonderful."

When the Quakers arrived, the Finns had begun to return in large numbers to the dearest place on earth to all men, their homeland, which Finns unshakably believe has a destiny to fulfill for mankind.

Their homes were in ruins, and their property was destroyed. Their gnawing physical hunger was great and constant; although inured from birth to Arctic cold, they now shivered through the winter with clothing meager or wholly inadequate. Even greater than the suffering from these privations seemed that from their terrible spiritual loneliness. Once when members of the Quaker work camp at Autti hastily built a crude stretcher between two bicycles on which to carry a farmer's child threatened with blood poisoning to a doctor, the father said, "I had forgotten there were kind people in the world." Except for the Swedes, all of their old friends seemed to have forgotten them. Their great and good friend and national ideal, the United States, against which they neither declared war nor fired a shot, had not lifted so much as a finger in their behalf, in spite of the continued urging and pleading of Herbert Hoover.

Even though they could say as did Job of old, "I have kept my integrity," they found it more difficult to say, even in their profound, simple faith, with Job, "The Lord giveth and the Lord taketh away. Blessed be the name of the Lord!"

Then suddenly, almost miraculously to them, the helping hand of friendship reached out from great America and touched them. They had yearned earnestly for such a confirmation of their faith. Because they are a proud and courageous people, they never had asked for it except in their most secret prayers. Finn after Finn reiterated to me that the Quaker help was all the more deeply appreciated because "you gave it without our asking for it."

The impartial Quakers, who have performed humanitarian service in nearly all the great and small nations of the world, play no favorites; neither race, color, creed, nor nationality can call on their special sympathies. They seek to submerge their dislikes and to make no sign of preference. Nevertheless, Quaker workers are human, and the Finns have captured their hearts.

Innumerable lakes, unending forests, and a limited amount of good productive soil (less than a tenth of Finland's area can be so classified) compel her people, not only for their well-being but for their very existence, to exercise thrift and industry. Both are dear to Quaker hearts.

The great natural beauty: an untold wealth of pines and hemlocks hemming in the countless lakes; here and there groups of birches, their white bodies lovely as children's playing naked in the sun; the unbroken masses of forest; the long days of summer and the crystalline seas of snow in winter; the stratopheric solitude—all these cast a spell and leave their mark on the Finnish character.

Nature, on the other hand, is in some respects a miser with Finland. The country, for example, has few wild creatures, animals or birds. Reindeer are numerous in some areas. Many of them crossed the highway or browsed in near-by woods while we traveled in the north country. They were somewhat shy of people but could not really be called wild. We saw none of the bears which live in the Lapland province woods. Once we saw a mother grouse hurrying her brood of tiny youngsters into the protective bushes at the edge of a woods.

My hurried glimpses found only meager evidence of the existence of birds and wild flowers in Finland. Her crows, gray-backed and a trifle larger than the American variety, do not *caw*. The Finnish blackbird is somewhat larger than his American cousin, and his black coat is flecked with patches of white. There are many small, nervous, quick-moving road runners with black eye rims, black breasts and crests, and grayish back and wings; they seem to skim their food from the air. I heard a few notes of song sparrows, but saw none of the singers. This scarcity of birds, and their silence in vast woodland stretches, during summer months, was in strange contrast with the unending, full-throated, joyous concerts one hears from nature's singers in our own forests in the summer and in the forests of South America during our winter months.

Also, nature is miserly with wild flowers in Finland.

Yet, in places, brilliant fireweed, white yarrow, Queen Anne's lace, and many buttercups, bluebells, mustard, and the ubiquitous dandelion flourish in profusion. In some forests, lilies of the valley grow in great clusters, and there is a wild rose with beautiful pink and white blossoms. Perhaps because of their comparative scarcity, the Finn loves flowers even more than most of us. In the southern windows of homes the war spared, one sees blooming begonias, fuchsias, nasturtiums, and geraniums. Since several thousand homes are to be built in Finland to replace those which, with their flowers and all other contents, the enemy destroyed, here is an opportunity for some American organization to make a gesture of fine friendship. To supply the homes of Finland with such seeds, slips, and bulbs as may be shipped would make an exceedingly satisfying, albeit small, contribution to a deep desire of the northerner. Otherwise such luxuries as a geranium at the casement will have to wait.

There is no method of determining exactly how much of the Finnish character is attributable to the opulence of nature on the one hand and her miserliness on the other, and how much to the morals and ideals of the Finns' religion. These unspoiled people, who live close to nature, look upon their God somewhat as an intimate friend who hears and understands their presentation of problems and hopes when they talk to Him in their prayers. "Thank you, God, for good food," said a little schoolboy at Kemijärvi, after the Quaker feeding began. His natural response serves to indicate the intimate and reverent attitude of Finns toward their Maker.

An intimacy with all life about him is characteristic of the Finn. Once when a Quaker field worker was making a sleigh trip to a distant village, she asked the driver to hurry his horse since they were late. Afterward, when she had sunk back into the blankets, she heard the driver say to his steed, "Hurry up, please trot some, little horse. Summer will soon come and then you can have a long rest." Another time a staff member sought to engage a Finn to move some supplies with his horse and cart, but the Finn said he could not because "my horse is having his vacation in the woods." This attitude is in keeping with the Finn's deliberate habits, both mental and physical. One hears there, time and again, the phrase, "God made no hurry in Lapland."

Two other qualities of Finnish character have been accentuated by their surroundings. One is that of sincere neighborliness, quite similar to that of our old West of unlocked homes, ready welcome to visitors, and genuine concern for the welfare of everyone. The other quality is openness of heart. Just as great distances and few people made for a frank friendliness in our old West, so they do in Finland. Yet this limitless expanse of their outlook and action, this quality of staking all, has its limitations. They are, for example, ultracautious in some ways. This may be due, in part, to their difficult existence and their many troubles. They are more than a little distrustful of outsiders.

Climatic conditions seem to have given the Finns some of the bear's great, lumbering movement, his strength, his ability to live on little and to remain awake around the clock in summer and sleep around it in winter. The spaciousness of nature in their land seems to give them spacious ideas of life; its solitude begets solitude of spirit and makes the Finn deeply religious. It helps also to explain why he clings to the timeless virtues of hope, courage, and integrity. "A man's given word is as much a part of him as are the horns of an ox," runs an old Finnish proverb.

The world, and particularly America, is especially conscious of the Finn's integrity. When many of the world's great nations defaulted on their debt payments to our government, Finland alone met principal and interest promptly and without complaint. It is true, as some say disparagingly, that Finland's indebtedness was not great. It is equally true that Finland's resources were slender, and that she desperately needed every cent for her own economic and social program in the years following her independence. It is further and everlastingly true that integrity is a question of quality, not quantity. The quality of Finland's integrity is not open to disparagement as is shown by a historical footnote given me by Dr. Raymond Moley. According to Moley the Roosevelt administration in 1933 was facing a serious international situation through the failure of foreign governments to meet their obligations to the United States. Mighty Britain made a token payment of ten cents on the dollar on her account. The French, Italians, and others not only paid nothing whatever but did not even write to ask for an extension of time on which to make a token payment. It was evident that international anarchy in finance would prevail unless steps were taken to get these defaulting governments on a current paying basis. Since most of the defaulting nations were experiencing financial difficulties, President Roosevelt and his undersecretary of state, Dr. Moley, decided that they should explore the possibility of getting payments made if the obligations were scaled down.

They recognized, however, that such a plan would meet with considerable public opposition unless it were presented to the American people in the most favorable manner. That could be done, they decided, by opening discussions and making such arrangements with the one nation in the world which would not arouse popular resentment. That nation was Finland.

This decision made, Dr. Moley met with the Finnish minister and stated that the government of the United States was ready to discuss with him a proposal for scaling down both interest and principal payments on the Finnish debt. Much to Moley's surprise the minister of Finland replied that the subject was not open to discussion; that his government would meet its obligations in full on the dates when they came due. The proposal was dropped when the Roosevelt-Moley lead-off man, the Finnish minister, refused even to discuss it.

Ravaged by war and disease, largely forgotten or ignored by their old friends, the Finns today are wholly occupied in rebuilding homes and struggling for existence. So is it, too, with the evacuees of Lapland, now back at home, whose sawmills are running ceaselessly to produce lumber for reconstruction, who are rebuilding and raising food. In the summer of 1946 they were busy literally day and night. The midnight sun made this possible. At Rovaniemi, in July, they had rebuilt 266 buildings and were at work on 486 more. In the rural districts the people have completed the work of rebuilding 16 per cent of the homes and other structures and are busy getting another 31 per cent finished before winter. They had repaired 72 per cent of the destroyed bridges and 50 per cent of the culverts.

Most of this work is being done by hand with small tools. Except at the site of the German-destroyed great railroad and highway bridge near Kemi, I did not see, either idle or busy, a single bulldozer, power shovel, cement mixer, or derrick in all Lapland. Even so the work of rebuilding has moved ahead fast. The Finn is an all-around, competent workman who seems able to run a worn-out truck with little more than baling wire and charcoal. He can do almost anything with his *puuka,* a large sheath knife with a wide blade which almost every male Finn carries fastened to his belt. It is an all-service tool, used for building boats, fitting lumber for homes, making shelters or fires, cutting bread, killing and dressing reindeer, or carving up a fellow Finn. I asked one Finn which he valued most, his wife or his knife. He thought a moment and replied with a seriousness which was probably assumed, "I don't know. Both are valuable."

In 1917 Finland started with little more than bare hands and *sisu.* There is no English synonym for *sisu.* It means courage, tenacity, stubbornness, determination, energy, and the ability and willingness to travel the last mile. These marked qualities of the Finn, stimulated perhaps by a hard soil, severe climate, and adverse destinies, plus the vast expanse of nature and the solitude of their existence, inspire them to undertake and accomplish the seemingly impossible. Old in antecedents, Finland is young in courage, vigor, and determination.

Faced with short summers, long, cold winters, few natural resources, and a limited amount of good soil, the Finns, nevertheless, have created a distinctive civilization of high quality, made a recognized place for their country in the family of nations. Difficulties and dangers fill their days, but they seem never to lose their faith and hope for a brighter future, or the love of a land which nature has treated with so little generosity. The road of these valiant people through history—the suffering, heavy sacrifices, and hard labor—has been sustained by the words of one of their greatest poets:

> I saw a people who their all
> Could yield: save honor glorious . . .
> Saw troops in frost and hunger thrall,
> That yet could fight victorious.

CHAPTER III

Selecting a Relief Project

IN THE WINTER of 1941 one of the members of the board which directs the American Friends Service Committee began to feel a "concern" for far-off Finland. Peculiarly sensitive spiritual antennae appear to enable many Quakers to discover, long before such situations become generally known, suffering and human need.

The Quaker on whose spirit the concern for Finland weighed heavily was Dr. Douglas V. Steere, professor of philosophy at Haverford College. This professorship was previously held by Dr. Rufus M. Jones, world-revered Quaker leader, the founder and until recently the chairman, and always the guiding spirit, of the American Friends Service Committee. This relationship of Steere with Dr. Jones, coupled with the fact that he had visited the subarctic nations of western Europe and had come to admire their sturdy, unspoiled people, made it natural for him to feel this concern.

Soon after the cessation of military hostilities in Europe made a relief program for Finland possible, the

Committee united with Steere in his concern to the
extent of asking him to investigate conditions in that
country. As soon as the college year of 1945 ended, he
flew first to Stockholm and later to Lapland. He in-
spected the devastated areas and went on to Helsinki,
where, as in Stockholm and Lapland, he conferred with
government officials, relief workers, and other leaders
concerned with Finland's chief problem.

Dr. Steere spent five months in the two countries,
from June to October 1945. To his colleagues in Philadelphia he made regular reports on conditions, needs,
and possible co-operation. The thoroughness of his investigation and his understanding approach are best
shown by some excerpts from these reports.

In an early letter he wrote:

Finland needs spiritual help to face her dismay and
despair. . . . The Finns are spiritually confused because of
attack by both sides during the war. It seems that an impartial carrier of good will would be a true aid in this
complex situation. It is a place where we might use some
of our able young personnel who long to have a chance to
meet need. . . . The Swedish authorities have given me every
conceivable courtesy and would be greatly heartened if
we saw fit to undertake something. President Judge Eke-
berg [head of the over-all Swedish foreign relief organ-
ization] gave me a most helpful hour last week. Folke
Bernadotte is keen to have us undertake some work in
Finland and the American minister was most encouraging.
I spent three hours going over our statements of motivation
and principle with Waris, the Finnish Secretary, who is
hungry for something beyond professional relief. We had a
moving conversation. . . . Here is a situation where more
than the commodities are needed although we cannot go
emptyhanded to people in their need.

Everywhere the cry is for clothing and shoes. Story after

story has come to me about families of six, seven and eight children—with one or two pair of wearable shoes. . . .

If AFSC decides to undertake this work I believe two men and one woman could easily handle the supply side. There is a maximum of cooperation over here from officials. . . . If we do decide to undertake it the first man should be despatched at once so that we could over-lap some.

Before Dr. Steere went to Finland, he had conferred at length in Stockholm with American, Swedish, and Finnish officials and with heads of relief organizations (Sweden, through government appropriations and private charity, had been carrying almost alone the burden of a tremendous program of relief in Finland) who informed him that northern Finland seemed to be the area most in need of help.

On August 1, 1945, Dr. Steere made his first full-length report to the Service Committee. It set forth, with clarity and completeness, the desperate need of the Finnish people and the extraordinary opportunity to render human service. To any non-Quaker it would give detailed evidence of both the spiritual attitude and the realism with which the Service Committee approaches the selection and the planning of a major relief project.

Dr. Steere pointed out:

Finland a year after the cessation of hostilities is in a period of transition between war and peace. Every industry, every available credit abroad, every conceivable export of wood or other products is being mobilized and devoted almost exclusively to the critical goal of her payment of reparations to Russia. This means that there is no unemployment to speak of now in Finland, but it means at the same time that she has felt it necessary to subordinate any adequate attempt to deal with the acute shortages of

food, clothing, foot-wear, and housing to this all-absorbing
task of meeting her heavy reparation payments on which
her very national existence depends. . . .

Steere then recited the shortage of consumer goods,
the destruction in Lapland, the Karelian evacuee problem and food needs, citing 1,171 calories per day as the
existing basic ration.

Clothing, he reported, was almost nonexistent except
for poor cellulose substitutes and some reconditioned
army clothing. Finland had had little new clothing since
1939. "The children who wear out and outgrow their
clothing so fast are in the worst condition of all."

The most severe needs [he wrote] however, are among
those who had to leave their homes hurriedly and have no
stock of laid-away things to tide them over. This has happened twice to 420,000 Karelians who were first driven out
of their homes in 1940 and then for a second time in 1944,
and it has happened at least once to the people who lived
in Northern Finland who were forced to evacuate hurriedly in the German retreat in the autumn of 1944 when
they could take with them little more than they carried
on their backs. Some of these had previously lost everything in the destruction of their homes in the winter war
in 1940. What gifts of clothing those evacuated inside
Finland got last winter and spring are now largely worn
out and warm clothing for the winter ahead where the
temperature reaches 20-30 degrees below zero Fahrenheit
is urgently demanded. . . .

All that was said of clothing goes for the matter of foot-
wear. Since 1939 there has been only a trickle of new all-
leather footwear available to anyone except workers in the
woods and in heavy industry and the soldiers in the army.
Women and children wear wooden soled shoes and clogs
in the summer. . . . These wooden shoes are hardly navigable
on ice or in snow. . . .

Finland has always had to import her sole leather because Finnish cattle hides are too thin-skinned to make suitable soles but are usable chiefly for uppers. The composition material used for soling shoes lasts on the average from 3 to 4 weeks. With the help of Sweden and their own hides for uppers, Finland if all surplus army shoes are counted in, has on hand a stock of shoes to be issued against special licenses for this next winter of less than 1 pair to each 3 children, 1 pair to each 5 women and less than 1 pair to each 3 men....

Steere also investigated housing facilities, which were appallingly inadequate due to the German destruction in Lapland plus the needs of the 450,000 evacuees from Porkkala, Petsamo, and Karelia areas which were ceded to Russia. According to him:

... the bulk of this surplus population must remain (1) quartered in the houses of the rest of the population which means sleeping often 6, 8 and even 10 in a room; or (2) crowded into temporary barracks in the North; or (3) living in tiny bathhouses, barns, cellars, or improvised shelters as in the North. All of this acute crowding means quite apart from the personal discomfort, lack of privacy, inadequate rest at night, etc., a greatly increased vulnerability to all contagious diseases. Epidemics of diphtheria, scarlet fever, and all children's diseases were frequent last winter and the infection of whole families by a single open case of tuberculosis is too common to provoke any great notice. "Tuberculosis in Finland today is a housing problem" a leading Finnish physician declared to me....

The shortage of railroad rolling stock and the poor condition of roadbed and bridges created a bottleneck in housing construction. Russia had taken as reparations payments 3,500 freight cars and 100 locomotives. These, when subtracted from the inadequate numbers left in the wake of German destruction, placed the burden of transporting housing materials on Finland's small fleet of four-year-old trucks, which were powered by charcoal because of the lack of gasoline.

The building program was also made difficult by the acute shortage of nails, window glass, cement, building iron. Nails, for example, were being sold singly in the black market. I saw men, women, and children sifting the ashes where their homes had stood, looking for nails and finding an occasional one. The Storm Troopers destroyed everything that could serve a human purpose in an area comprising 60,000 square miles. Houses, barns, machinery, livestock, fences, fishing tackle—everything fell to their torches or was mined. Time after time I was warned by staff members or Finnish friends to keep out of the woods and fields because of the thousands of unexploded hidden mines.

According to the Medical Division of the Finnish Red Cross the people of Finland were in need of fat-containing food, like cod-liver oil, which contained the principal vitamins required by people in the far north. Later the field workers asked for vitamin tablets from America.

In Rovaniemi, Dr. Steere wrote, three thousand men, women, and children had returned to sleep in cellars, sheds, cardboard tents, automobile bodies, and in the few barracks that had begun to appear.

The church, school and court of justice [he reported] have all used the same two rooms. Some of the large cement buildings are being repaired, the hospital is being worked at and an improvised school is being erected for fall occupancy, but the desperate shortage of building materials and of transport makes the hope of any serious rebuilding of dwelling houses impossible for next summer....

Public officials, school teachers, doctors in Rovaniemi

and Red Cross officials in Kemi are all worn down by the magnitude of their tasks and the long grinding years of the war. Nerve tiredness and in many cases almost apathy is the order of the day. The result is that any extra duty or new undertaking if they are to bear the responsibility for it seems impossible to them and they reject it. The only thing that carries them along is the hope of better days next year. . . .

Yet with all of this there is the faith that if they can get through this next winter they will be able to rebuild and to be in a much stronger position in the fall of 1946. This will-to-live and will to rebuild is a heroic thing to see. One woman that I met had had her home burned down three times in the last five years, first in the Winter war, then by Russian partisans in 1943 and having managed to get it up again, it was then destroyed by the Germans in 1944. Yet she is bound to return and rebuild it for a fourth time!

Dr. Steere next examined the possibilities of outside relief for Finland during the winter and summer of 1945–46. His report to the Committee expressed the opinion that Swedish relief must still remain the principal foreign help to Finland and that indications were that this aid would continue in fair volume.

He pointed out also that UNRRA had been officially requested by the Finnish government to give aid in the territory which had been devastated by the Germans during the period when the Finns were engaged in a war against Germany on the Allied side. Finnish officials, Steere reported, had listed all of their needs for relief and rehabilitation. These placed special emphasis upon the shortage of motor trucks and tires and on getting substantial assistance in securing the building material for reconstruction. But the UNRRA Council meeting in London in August of 1945 took no action, and only in December 1945 upon the insistent urging of Herbert Hoover's friends did it decide to help Finland with a grant of two and one-half million dollars. This assistance did not actually reach Finland until the 1945–46 winter was over. But it did arrive and was of enormous assistance to the province of Lapland during the winter of 1946–47. Its arrival also made it possible for the Quakers to concentrate their 1946–47 winter's efforts in hard-pressed central Finland.

The American Red Cross began a program in Finland in the fall of 1945 and has rendered most substantial aid there, particularly in regions where the Karelian evacuees are massed, It has sent and distributed large amounts of clothing, babies' layettes, bed clothing and shoes, drugs and hospital supplies to all sections of Finland.

After discussions with Finnish officials, Dr. Steere presented for consideration a proposal that the Service Committee carry out a supplemental feeding program at provisional village schools in Lapland. This proposal was conditional on the Finnish government's furnishing, through established subsidy, such rough staples as oatmeal and potatoes. The Quakers were to furnish milk, cod-liver oil, sugar for porridge, and certain meats and fats for soup. The Service Committee was also to supply facilities for cooking wherever such were needed. Before making his recommendations, Dr. Steere had ascertained that fifty tons of powdered milk and five to ten tons of cod-liver oil could be purchased in Sweden and that it seemed possible to arrange for the purchase of $25,000 worth of soup fats and some sugar in Denmark.

In discussing the question of field personnel, Dr. Steere expressed the belief that a condition which would make the program most effective would be that of the inspiring effect upon the Finns of a half a dozen fresh, strong, able workers who possessed a variety of skills and bold resourcefulness. "Such a group," Finnish officials told him, "would give us hope and courage to go on."

A final proposal [Steere wrote] is that the Quakers provide the centers with a limited emergency transport consisting of four vehicles. These would be almost indispensable in covering so large a territory and in getting food supplies placed promptly. They could also assist the Finnish relief distributing agency in emergency cases where acute shortages were discovered and other regular transport had broken down as is reported to be often the case, and they could keep link with Haparanda, Sweden, the border point to which the school-feeding supplies will be shipped.

Six months service from a business administrator moving in Scandinavia would be necessary to organize and procure Scandinavian supplies for this program and a young associate director should be provided who could carry on throughout the year.... Foreign Minister Svento and Social Affairs Minister Kilpi have given assurances that no difficulties are foreseen in securing Finnish visas for the entry of the American personnel and American observer, Maxwell Hamilton, who is thoroughly acquainted with the above proposals sees no difficulty in the presence of such a group of American Quaker Relief workers in Finland at this time providing no uniforms are worn and the State Department agrees.

Dr. Steere validated the recommendations contained in this and other reports and in his letters with strongly supporting letters from the Swedish Quakers who "heartily approved the proposed Finnish project," and from Unno Hannula, governor of Lapland; Heikki Waris, executive director of Suomen Huolto (Finnish

Relief); Sigfrid Sirenius, founder of Settlement movement in Finland; the Rev. Aarvo Ohinen, operations
chairman of Rovala Settlement and director of Finnish
Red Cross in Lapland; the Rev. Aaro Tolso, settlement
worker in Lapland for nineteen years.

Eight months after the relief program, which he
sponsored, had been initiated, Aarvo Ohinen, in a public statement, said:

The people of Lapland, in little Finland, are very grateful for the aid which has come from America through the
American Friends Service Committee. In two ways we have
felt this help has been more significant than most relief
work.

First, this aid has come without our asking for it, with
the warm love of our brothers in America. Second, with
this help came individuals—our friends—who gave themselves. Clothing given by loving hands is warm, indeed. It
also warms the soul.

We have needed the clothing and shoes very much in the difficult circumstances in which we are living. But just as
important has been the spiritual influence.

As for the child feeding, we feel that the growing generation has been saved for life; and our children are the most
important and the most valuable riches of our Lapland.
This aid from abroad has encouraged us to strain our own
resources to the utmost, to help ourselves....

Our memories of this aid, which we are receiving in the
days of our great distress, will last from generation to
generation. Mother will tell daughter, father will tell son,
throughout the years.

CHAPTER IV

A Stirring to Action in Philadelphia

THE Foreign Service Executive Committee of the Service Committee, after considering Dr. Steere's reports regarding the existing needs in Finland and his recommendations as to the nature of the proposed relief, stated that it "approved of the conditions under which a program for Finland might properly be established, subject to approval by the Board of Directors."

The Committee added that since a relatively small program was envisaged, work might be concentrated in the Lapland province, where needs were most acute, where the ration allowance then was 1,187 calories per day—less than half the amount required to maintain life and health in cold climates—and where unrationed supplements, such as potatoes and fish, were practically unobtainable. The Committee reported its findings to the Board of Directors and recommended that the larger body approve Douglas Steere's recommendations.

In dealing with other factors in the problem, it expressed the belief that approximately eight persons would be needed: an administrator; a person to handle the purchase and expediting of shipments from Sweden, Denmark, etc.; and six workers to carry on at the local level. The personnel office felt that it could meet this need. There was also a possibility that a Swedish Friend might be willing to serve in a liaison capacity.

The Committee further recommended that the extent of the program to be undertaken at that time should be as follows:

Clothing and shoes	$82,500.00
Foods	85,500.00
Transport	20,000.00
Housing (barracks)	9,500.00
Personnel	42,900.00
Philadelphia overhead	9,600.00
	$250,000.00

In addition, the Committee set forth the following conditions and recommendations as basic to the program:

1. We must have help of government in obtaining supplies and shipping space. The Swedish-American line has already offered free space, and the War Relief Control Board is inquiring of the War Shipping Administration. The War Relief Control Board will assist us in our effort to obtain from the Foreign Economic Administration needed allocations of goods for export.

2. All money for the program, including administrative charges, must be raised outside the normal fund-raising channels of the Committee. For certain technical reasons the War Relief Control Board is unable to license any Finnish-American group. However, it is willing to have us authorize Help Finland, Inc., a New York corporation, to raise money under our license. A second corporation composed of other Finnish-American groups was also recognized as a fund-raising agency under the Service Com-

mittee's license [The leaders of these two Finnish-American groups had been active workers in the Finnish Relief Fund efforts in 1939–40 which Herbert Hoover organized and directed. Now, as in 1940, Mr. Hoover helped to get them organized to raise money for the Quaker program. His interest now was a twofold one; need of his good friends the Finns, and support of the Service Committee, in which he has long been interested and to which he has brought much financial support.]

The Swedish Legation, Department of Finnish Interests, is now holding $110,000 for Finnish relief collected in the campaign of 1939–40 [the Legation's unexpended balance of the $4,000,000 Finnish Relief Fund raised in 1939–40 by Mr. Hoover] and has expressed an intention to the War Relief Control Board of turning the bulk of this money over to us if the Board of Directors of AFSC authorizes the acceptance of responsibility for a program in Finland. This money would be immediately available pending the raising of further funds by the Finnish-Americans. There are also funds, approximately $25,000, held in custody by Finnish Relief Fund, Inc., New York which would probably be made available to AFSC if a program is undertaken.

3. The AFSC should select the personnel.

4. The publicity in connection with fund-raising must follow the AFSC's general policies as to need, program and grounds of appeal.

Reasons for AFSC undertaking the program

Apart from the question of need, the staff believes that the following factors are of significance in considering whether or not a program should be launched at this time in Finland:

1. The AFSC is the only group which the President's War Relief Control Board is willing to license to do this job at the present time.

2. At the present date neither UNRRA nor the National

War Fund has shown an interest in Finland, and any action by these groups would be too late for this winter. The Swedish official help will be continued but it is limited. Swedish private agency help is limited because of the elimination from Swedish tax laws of credits for charitable gifts.

3. Normal channels of trade are not open to the Finns and such help as she receives from Russia is offset by her reparations payments to Russia.

4. Finland is a favorable locale for our first relationships with the Russians.

5. The Finns are spiritually confused because of attack by both sides during this War. A personal relationship in the giving of material relief therefore assumes greater significance and may provide an opportunity to lessen Russo-Finnish tensions. It seems to us that an impartial carrier of good will would be a true aid in this complex relationship. All of the elements just mentioned are present in our statements of principles for selecting foreign work adopted by the Committee last December.

These conditions were all met in due course and opened the way for the Board of Directors to authorize the launching of a relief program in Finland. In the meantime the Foreign Service Committee had been active in exploring the possibilities for co-operation with governments and private groups, and in selecting personnel.

The Foreign Service Executive Committee minutes show that on August 27, 1945, James Andrews, a graduate of Haverford College and a young Unitarian lawyer in Philadelphia, who was a member of the Service Committee's staff, quoted a letter from the President's War Relief Control Board which indicated that a voluntary relief program for Finland could be formalized if the American Friends Service Committee requested that its license be amended to extend its lawful activities.

Quoting from a report of the Foreign Service Executive Committee, these amendments were as follows:

1) Extension and distribution of voluntary relief funds and supplies to the people of Finland. Acceptance of responsibility as the single facilitating agency to this end until March 1, 1946, unless conditions demand the registration and license by the President's War Relief Control Board of an additional agent or agencies.

2) Acceptance of funds or contributions in kind:

   a) Available funds of Suomen Huolto (Finnish Relief) held in custody by the Swedish Legation, on behalf of the Finnish authorities.
   b) Available funds held in custody by Finnish Relief Fund, Inc., New York.
   c) Funds and contributions in kind from Help Finland, Inc., or any other organizations specified as agents of the American Friends Service Committee and so recorded with the President's War Relief Control Board in accordance with regulations 501.6 and 501.7: Provided that, not to exceed $150,000 in funds may be accepted from such agents without further authority from the President's War Relief Control Board. Contributions in kind without limitation as to monetary value.

This would provide for Finnish-Americans to raise money under our license. The date, March 1, 1946, provides for an opportunity to review the situation at that time and does not mean a termination of any relief work contemplated.

The $150,000 ceiling on fund raising was considered to be undesirable.

The Committee directed the staff to negotiate for removal of this clause, or, if this is not possible, an increased amount, or lacking either, a clear understanding that the Committee has the privilege of requesting an increase at a later date. [This was done.]

The Committee approved the suggested amendment to our license as noted above and felt that this minute should be added to its former recommendations to the Board.

On September 21, 1945, the Service Committee announced in a news release that it would conduct a relief project in Finland. James Andrews accepted the call to duty and flew to Stockholm on September 29 in time to meet Douglas Steere there and get his help and guidance in taking the next step in applying the relief program for Finland.

Quaker hearts were now easy, because the Finnish plan met fully their usual basic requirements in the selection of a relief project. These are: (1) an area of great need which other relief agencies, for whatever reason, have neglected; (2) adverse conditions which make operations difficult; (3) a people who need friendship as much as they need food, clothing, and medicine; (4) strong ideological crosscurrents which challenge the Quaker determination to project their service above creed, color, nationality, and ideology.

CHAPTER V

Support for a Quaker Project

As BEFORE stated the public at large, both in the United States and abroad, give Quakers far more credit for their humanitarian services than is their rightful due. The Service Committee's relief work in Finland is a case in point. In this project, aside from the activities of its field staff, it acted largely as a clearing house and as a purchasing and distributing agent for the Finnish-American groups. Dr. Steere's recommendations for the program were largely based upon the information, invaluable advice, and other help of such men as Count Bernadotte, head of the Swedish Red Cross, Dr. Heikke Waris of the Finnish United Relief, and a host of other Swedish and Finnish officials as well as of our own consular and diplomatic representatives in Sweden and Finland.

SHIPPING HELP

For example, a special contribution enabled the American Friends Service Committee to ship, freight free, a total of 551 tons of food, clothing, ready-to-erect barracks, seeds, and other supplies to Rovaniemi, Finland, from the United States, Sweden, and Denmark. Upon their reaching Rovaniemi, these goods, without cost to the Quakers, were then delivered to 268 communities scattered throughout Finnish Lapland, a territory approximately 200 miles wide and 300 miles long.

The Quakers thus could use the contributions of Finnish-Americans and other groups and individuals directly for the purchase of supplies making each contributed dollar produce one hundred cents' worth of supplies. Though equivalent to an actual contribution of tens of thousands of dollars, the regular ocean, railway, and truck haulage costs do not appear in the Committee's budget of $350,000 in cash, plus an equal sum in kind for Finnish relief.

Nearly three hundred tons of American food and supplies were carried from New York to Göteborg without charge. The Swedish national railways picked up these supplies at Göteborg and hauled them all the way across Sweden to Haparanda on the Swedish-Finnish border. The Swedish railways also hauled to Haparanda, and again without charge, the entire remainder of approximately 250 tons of Quaker supplies bought in Denmark and Sweden.

The Finnish national railways in turn picked up these 551 tons of supplies at Haparanda and in the same helpful, neighborly spirit hauled them without charge to Rovaniemi. And the Finnish Red Cross with its trucks also came into the picture at Rovaniemi and played the last act in this drama of generosity by hauling 551 tons of lifesaving supplies to communities all over the province of Lapland.

Great credit for the success of the Service Committee's

work in Finland must go, therefore, to these four organizations for their generous contributions in service, which translated into dollars represent a large sum.

MATERIAL HELP

Many other organizations also contributed services and goods which do not appear in the modest Quaker budget for Finland. For example, a co-operative society in Massachusetts gave 2,700 pounds of seed potatoes. All clothing except children's shoes was collected largely by Finnish-Americans in the States, without cost to the Quakers. At a conservative estimate its value was over $300,000.

One American firm gave the Service Committee seven million vitamin tablets, which Finnish medical authorities believe did as much to bring the children through the winter in good shape as did even the supplemental food. The long winters with little sunshine tend to pull the children down, making them especially susceptible to skin eruptions and other diseases. The spring of 1946 found large numbers of Finnish children in good shape despite undernourishment, inadequate clothing, and undesirable housing—thanks in no small part to these vitamins, the medical authorities contend.

By coincidence the vitamins, white in color, were wrapped in blue paper—the colors of the Finnish flag. These colors, plus the sugar-coating on the vitamins, made them particularly popular. Today, all over Lapland, one sees every now and then a bit of that vital blue paper fluttering in the wind.

SERVICE HELP

Although the Quaker personnel in Finland, all volunteer, never exceeded ten, the number of volunteer workers on the Committee's project exceeded five hundred.

One factor which made it possible for the staff to move quickly and surely in organizing and carrying out their program was that the Finnish people have a well-developed talent for organization and co-operation. Although the Finns were shattered economically, depressed spiritually, and confused socially, their organizing ability, a dominant characteristic of a superior people, responded readily and effectively.

An UNRRA representative, commenting on this quality, said that he accomplished more in Finland in two weeks than in six months in one southern and again in one central European country.

The Finns, moreover, never were whipped. Some deep inner spiritual source renewed their hope and fed their determination to go forward. This was fortified by the arrival of long and tragically needed help. Shortly after the Quaker workers arrived in Rovaniemi, one Finn, deeply moved, said to them, "You are relieving our greatest need, lack of food for our children. They must have it. We grownups can get along some way, but our little folks cannot. We have been so sure for a long time that you Americans would come. Now this is our happiest day. It can be the beginning of a thousand years of peace which we all long for so much."

The appreciative attitude of this man was typical of that held by everyone. As a natural result Finns, individually and collectively, turned to and gave ready service to help the Americans.

Suomen Huolto, the over-all Finnish relief organization, whose membership includes that of twenty-one national Finnish relief organizations, has helped to solve every official, personnel, and public problem which the Quakers have faced.

The twenty Finnish health sisters (public health nurses) in Lapland, gave the Quaker workers willing co-operation which took much of their time.

The school inspectors of Lapland as well as the teachers in 268 schools—many of the schools have two or more teachers—helped the Quaker workers without stint. Worthy of special mention is the fact that they cooked and served the food which the Service Committee furnished the school children. In many cases, war, the wrecker, had destroyed stoves, kettles, and other equipment used by the schools in cooking and serving meals. The Quakers provided new equipment, but it was the teachers who did the work. Among all the European individuals and groups who rose to the emergencies of a war without precedent for horror and a peace without parallel for suffering, none displayed finer qualities than the teachers of Finland. The war's material destruction left the country short of schoolhouses, and its carnage and displacements reduced the number of teachers. As a consequence, most of the schools carried on with two shifts of pupils—some of them with three. Now, to their daily grind of teaching overcrowded classes the teachers of Finnish Lapland added service as cooks, waitresses, and dishwashers. Their working day began at eight in the morning and ended at six in the evening. But in their burning eagerness to make tomorrow's Finland stronger and wiser they took all this in stride, without complaining or faltering.

The Finnish Settlement Association also co-operated

with the Quakers, finding interpreters and other volunter help as needed, plus giving invaluable advice.

Private and public medical organizations and authorities provided free services and hospitalization for all sick people whom the Quakers sent them. In addition, the Finnish Red Cross, with the help of army officials, delivered the food to the schools and distributed 173 tons of clothing and shoes to thirteen volunteer communal clothing committees created to allot these necessities to individuals in their areas. This clothing had been collected, repaired, and packed for shipment by American Finns.

Another large group which gave the Quakers free and full co-operation was that formed by officials of the communes where the Quakers worked. The services of local building masters were invaluable.

The Lappinnaa Co-operative restaurant fed without charge all staff workers who could not be cared for at the barracks, as they passed through Rovaniemi.

This catalogue of organized help to the Quakers does not include the much greater service given by individual Finns. Co-operation was universal and continuous. An illustration: Once a truck laden with Quaker goods broke down. That was a habit of those charcoal-powered trucks, but this time the driver could not get it going. Another truck came along, loaded with potatoes. It stopped, and the two men on the driver's seat helped until they found that their potatoes were in danger of freezing. They delivered them and returned, going several miles out of their way, and spent several more hours hammering and tinkering before the engine of the Quaker truck coughed and came to life. The Finns have a special knack of keeping their worn-out trucks bouncing over the highways.

Another service requiring considerable man and woman power which Finnish groups and individuals performed for the Service Committee was that of investigating complaints about distribution of food and clothing. Without exception all complaints were handled competently, courageously, and impartially, and all cause for future complaint removed.

Before the Quakers moved on any community, a member of the staff visited it for a preliminary survey. He appraised the need, estimated the necessary quantity of supplies, got acquainted with local officials, teachers, and other influential citizens. So, with the way cleared, the team which followed could get to work at once. This advance agent was always careful to explain the nature, motives, purposes, and extent of the work, so gaining complete and understanding co-operation. And when the supplies arrived, the workers made a new survey with the object of getting the first help to the most needy, especially those with the largest families.

Conditions in some places were indescribably bad. When the workers arrived in Savukoski, a town with a prewar population of a thousand, they found only one building, a barracks of postwar construction in which many families were living. Then people began emerging from the surrounding ruins. They were living in tiny cellars with dirt floors, which housed families including as many as seven children. The compelling urge to return to the sites of their ruined homes and build toward an unknown future is a marked characteristic of all Finns today.

In every cellar home they visited, the Quakers were offered coffee with accompaniments. The coffee was ersatz made of burned grains—Finland had no real coffee for six years. But the hosts made no apologies either for that or for the pathetic dearth of furniture, dishes, or food. They were dipping into tiny and precious hoards of this imitation coffee, of sugar, butter, and bread. Nevertheless, what they had was served as proudly as though theirs were a king's table. The Quakers scarcely had the heart to deprive them, yet they knew that refusal of such hospitality, offered in such a generous and friendly spirit, would not have been understood; and as they passed from cellar to cellar they often drank "coffee" to the bursting point. It was in these social visits that the Quakers recruited their army of volunteer workers.

FINANCIAL SUPPORT

As noted before, the handful of Quakers—about one out of every 1,200 people in the United States—cannot finance the world-wide activities which the American Friends Service Committee initiates and directs. Non-Quakers provide most of the money required to carry out such relief activities.

The source of funds to meet the cost of the Finnish project is a case in point. The Service Committee did meet the cost of the initial survey in Finland and that of investigating possible sources of money in the United States, of conferring with State Department officials, and of providing the literature which carried the information about the work and the need. All of this required only a few thousand dollars.

The first big financial help for the undertaking came from the Swedish Legation, Department of Finnish Interests, in Washington. It held $110,000 of frozen credits for Finnish relief which had been raised but not expended by the Hoover committee in 1939–40. The

Swedish Legation at the direction of the Finnish government unfroze $75,000 of this sum and turned it over to the Service Committee for use in purchasing relief supplies in America.

Herbert Hoover's former committee, Finnish Relief Fund, Inc., contributed $30,000 of its remaining funds. The Brethren Service Committee made different contributions, one of 120,000 pounds of Quaker Oats. The Goodwill Industries of Detroit contributed 15,346 cans of assorted vegetables, and the Church Committee on Overseas Relief added another 20,200 cans. The United Farmers Co-operative of Fitchburg, Massachusetts, gave $2,717.13 for the purchase of garden and vegetable seeds and the Foreign Mission Board of the Southern Baptist Church gave $2,500.

To raise money for this project, an all-Sibelius concert was given in New York. To this performance the great composer cabled:

I have noted with great joy how through the agency of the American Friends Service Committee sorely needed aid has been provided our war stricken people. It is heartwarming to realize that the Finnish Americans and indeed the great American public at large is behind this welfare work. I am happy about the concert arranged in my honor and its good purpose. Heartfelt thanks to the organizers, performers and audience for the attention thus given our beloved country.

Jan Sibelius

The Lutheran Church and the Church of the Brethren also made generous contributions to the Quaker fund.

However, Finnish-American groups are entitled to major credit; for they gave or secured most of the funds and goods which the Service Committee distributed.

Two of their organizations, Help Finland, Inc., and United Finnish Relief, Inc., raised the bulk of the Quakers' Finland budget and collected clothing as agents of the Friends Service Committee.

The Service Committee's arrangement with these groups was specified by the War Relief Control Board in Washington which for technical reasons was unable to license any Finnish-American group to raise money. The Board, however, was willing that the Service Committee should authorize such an organization to raise money under their license. This was done. Inasmuch as ideological differences existed in the Finnish-American population, the Quakers avoided possible complications by licensing two separate groups.

With policies and plans for the public appeal perfected, the Finnish-American groups organized committees and by devoted hard work raised nearly a quarter of a million dollars for the Quakers. Aside from the help of speakers, literature, and information supplied by the Service Committee, they did this almost singlehanded. Their work in America made it possible for the Committee's work in Finland to be great and useful. They are entitled to unqualified praise.

One Quaker dollar given to the Service Committee thus starts an endless chain of generosity, co-operation, and helpfulness which grows and grows until finally it is matched in goods and services with hundreds, even thousands, of non-Quaker dollars.

CHAPTER VI

Stockholm Office Activities

THE American Friends Service Committee has established certain working methods to be followed in all its projects.

One is that the program must remain flexible so that the field staff may make adjustments to it as circumstances require. This procedure emphasizes and explains in large measure why Quaker humanitarian activities are given such widespread support. The staff field workers chosen are superior men and women whose training and experience fully qualify them to deal competently with emergencies such as cannot be anticipated when the programs are initiated. Furthermore, the Quakers, in their efforts to help human beings in a human way, instinctively follow the leadings of their hearts and heads rather than blueprints which have been drawn in an office thousands of miles away.

A flexible program of this nature also is necessary from a practical point of view, and down-to-earth practicality is a marked Quaker quality. For instance, the Service Committee seldom knows at the time a program is initiated how much money may be contributed to support it. The size of the program at the beginning thus is fixed by the funds in hand plus whatever may reasonably be expected to come in. Despite this exercise of Quaker caution, the Committee plans and starts much of its relief work on faith and its own good commercial credit. When works (meaning contributions) support their faith, the field staff speeds up its helpful activities and increases their extent.

Even so this method of playing by heart and head—by ear, as it were—bogs down when applied to relief projects located far from America unless the Service Committee establishes supply points as near as possible to the base of operations. The supply point for the Lapland project was staked out in Stockholm in the early fall of 1945 by James Andrews of the Service Committee's Philadelphia staff. In addition to his having been exposed to Quaker ways and thinking all his life, Andrews had an excellent working knowledge of Service Committee procedures and philosophy. It now seems doubtful, in view of his record of accomplishments and the innumerable new friends he made for the Service Committee in Stockholm, that the Philadephia office could have selected a better man for the job than this open-faced, quiet-voiced, gently smiling, slender young man.

In his early thirties, with good health, a surplus of energy and ability, and a zeal to serve, Andrews quickly made an important place for himself and the Service Committee project in Swedish and Finnish official and relief circles. Months after he had left Stockholm, when I met these people, almost the first question they would ask was, "How is Jim Andrews?" Everywhere, at the American and Finnish Legations, in the

Swedish foreign office, the Swedish Red Cross, the Swedish European Relief, and at the offices of other relief organizations, one or more people would press me to carry warm greetings to him.

Shortly after he had reached Stockholm the warmth of his personality and the sincerity of his purpose, combined with the reasonableness of his requests, began to work their magic. Some of the men with whom he had worked most closely told me later that they always found it difficult to refuse any request he made. Thus he secured licenses to buy and ship goods, had full co-operation in speeding shipments, got visas readily, and handled with speed and without friction the countless and varied responsibilities of his office.

Andrews began operating without any office help whatever. Swedish Quakers provided him with a ten-by-fifteen-foot office space, heated by overflow warmth from a wood-burning stove in an adjoining room. He kept warm mainly with the help of activity and concentration. He found living quarters at a cost of twenty dollars a month, had a telephone installed in the office, put in some shelves to serve as filing cabinets, found a desk, bought a typewriter, and went to work.

By having his office at the Swedish Quaker Center, Andrews gained the advantage of assistance and advice from people who knew conditions in Finland. Thereby he avoided going against any pattern of theirs; also they helped him work out the most effective way of starting operations.

At the beginning Andrews spent a major part of every day seeing government officials. This was necessary because the success of the Finnish program rested upon good working relations with three governments: the Finnish, the Swedish, and the Danish. Therefore, he was not in a position to utilize the services of a secretary, assuming he could have found one. There was one other disadvantage to having a secretary at the start—the office was cold, because Sweden was then operating most heating facilities with wood. Andrews, who was moving around during the day, was not bothered by the cold. At night, he bundled up and did all of his own typing —such as reports to Philadelphia, requests to the Swedish government and Swedish relief officials, or reports on shipments to field workers. He cast up his accounts on Sundays.

As the project grew, he found that office work had begun to cut into his business day, thereby preventing his seeing officials as needed. This problem was solved when he met a French Quaker who had a Swedish wife. The couple had given a period of eight years' service to the British Quakers at a school which they operated in Madagascar, and were spending a furlough in Sweden. The man became Andrews' office factotum and proved to be a valuable help in taking care of office routine until the British Quakers sent him to work in the prisons in France. Andrews was able to find a substitute for him in a German refugee whom he met in Stockholm and who had a great interest in Quaker work. Also, he was effective as an office manager. As the office work increased and his outside activities speeded up accordingly, Andrews employed an UNRRA typist to work for him after hours.

The reason why the Finnish project was slow in getting under way was that when Andrews first arrived in Stockholm neither he nor the Philadelphia office knew definitely how much money would be available for the program. The Service Committee, because of its many commitments abroad, had undertaken the program originally with the understanding that Finnish-Americans would provide all of the funds. These Finnish-Americans, who in turn were just getting organized, were not able to use publicity channels until late fall, when the program finally had been cleared diplomatically. This was accomplished in October 1945. But unfortunately for them, that month brought a National War Fund Drive. The Finnish campaign had been planned too late to be included in this over-all effort. Then November brought the Victory Loan Drive; and so it was December before they could steam ahead under full power.

Finally, money-raising in the United States calls for a certain amount of ballyhoo. And Americans think in concrete terms. To rouse them, the collector for any cause needs incident, color, background. But the staff, the only agency available to supply such information in terms which we would understand, did not arrive on the scene until late in 1945. This factor slowed down the early operations of the Finnish-Americans.

But these were only delays. They did not alter the fundamental plan. And meantime no other relief work of any kind was going on in Lapland. The overworked American Red Cross had not yet got around to that remote area, and UNRRA did not move on Finland until March and April 1946. The help ultimately given to Finland by both of these organizations was of enormous assistance and supplemented in major ways the initial help of the Quakers. Because the Quakers were the first Americans to reach Finland, a great deal of publicity followed that first visit of Andrews and Dr. Steere to Helsinki. The Finns assumed that the Quakers were all ready to go ahead with the program and that the stage had been reached when there was real news for the Finnish people. He and Dr. Steere were extremely careful not to overdo publicity because success depended entirely upon how much money the Finnish-American group could raise. They were cautious about promising more than they could perform. Therefore, they discussed plans with the Finnish press at Helsinki in rather general terms; but they laid especial emphasis on the nature of the Quaker approach to work and the Quaker desire to do a small job well rather than to spread themselves out too thin. This initial publicity, showing as it did that volunteers of their kind had come so far to perform a friendly service, helped to create a feeling of good will.

The arrangement which the Quakers made with the American Red Cross assured full co-operation without duplication of effort. The Quakers were to work in Lapland while the Red Cross planned to operate mainly in southern Finland. Dr. Steere and Andrews, however, did have some difficulty in convincing officials of Suomen Huolto, who were responsible for the entire Finnish program of relief, that the Service Committee's work should initially be restricted to Lapland, which was in the greatest need, of manageable size for the Quaker staff, and within the fund-raising capacity of the Finnish-Americans.

In their first meeting with the officials of Suomen Huolto and in line with Dr. Steere's earlier recommendations, the two representatives of the Service Committee outlined a contract which would limit their activities to Lapland. Another agreement expressed a guiding principle of Quaker relief policy. The inhabitants should do a share of the job themselves. In line with this, the Finns agreed to provide the equipment necessary for feeding in the schools and certain basic foods, such as soup and cereal on alternate days, in order that American expenditure might be confined to purchasing certain foods high in caloric values which Finland did not have. Suomen Huolto officials undertook to stand all transportation costs, once the goods had reached the Finnish border, and to be responsible for the insurance thereof. Since they were the gift of the American people, they would enter customs free. The Quakers would have control of their distribution. Further, the work could be extended outside of the specified area only with the consent of the chief representative of the Service Committee. At a later date, Suomen Huolto officials further agreed to pay the expenses of the Quaker overhead in Finland such as travel, telephone, and Finnish food for the staff. After a few conferences which wasted little time, Steere and Andrews spent a night drawing up a contract embracing these terms and getting it translated. Next morning they submitted it to the Finnish authorities. By noon they announced to a press conference that the contracting parties had reached a tentative agreement.

The Quaker method of flexibility in relief work was aided in many ways by the establishment of the office in Stockholm. Seldom have the Quakers invaded a desert of want with an oasis so near as Sweden to Finland. Because of this proximity they could buy barracks material and get all necessary equipment, from teacups to roofing paper, through the co-operation of Swedish merchants. By the time these orders were placed, the snow had already begun to cover the ground in Lapland. Therefore it was necessary to get the barracks erected as rapidly as possible in order that the staff would not displace those permanent inhabitants whose wants they were relieving. Bringing such supplies from the United States would have slowed down the work by as much as two months. Also, the Stockholm office furnished food for the workers themselves. Naturally they did not wish to draw on the scant supply of local food. Also, since the workers must carry heavy burdens, it was necessary to keep them in good condition. It seemed best that these newcomers to a country with a severe climate and unfamiliar dietary habits should live, so far as possible, as they lived at home. If they consumed a share of the scant Finnish food, that was in the belief that it helped to make them more a part of the community.

The establishment of an office in Stockholm also helped greatly in solving transportation problems. The Swedish Army co-operated with the Service Committee by selling it two trucks, which it turned over to the Finnish Red Cross as its distribution agency in Finland. These trucks could not have been purchased from the United States Army stocks in France or elsewhere in time to carry out the program in Finland during the winter of '45–46.

From his fortunate situation in Stockholm, Andrews was able to purchase a great deal of powdered milk and margarine in Sweden and to import salted pork and sugar from Denmark. The feeding program was necessarily kept simple because of the lack of cooking utensils in Finland and also because it was imperative that the difficulties of distribution be held to a minimum in an Arctic winter. The diet, as planned, was to include the Quaker-purchased milk and sugar to go with the cereal that the Finns furnished, the salt pork in the soup, and margarine to make appetizing the crusts of bread which the children brought to school.

The Danes had a relatively stiff policy on export, and

when the field staff found that it was going to be equally
difficult to obtain beef or pork, it decided immediately
to concentrate upon pork since this had a higher caloric
content to the pound. The Danes were willing to sell
because they were interested in obtaining American
dollars at that time. The Bacon Board in Copenhagen
made every effort to treat and package the salt pork to
the most minute staff specifications. The pork was fresh,
because it was slaughtered on the day when the order
was placed. After three weeks for salting, it was shipped
to Finland in thirty- to fifty-kilo crates. These relatively
small containers were necessary because in many instances two men would be the sole motive power to
handle them at the terminal. Also, some schools had a
relatively small number of pupils, and the staff wanted
to break open as few cases as possible after they reached
the barracks in Lapland.

The job of obtaining supplies in Sweden required
constant attention. Once a strike threatened to endanger
the supply of powdered milk. Once again the Allies cut
down on the amount of fats and oils which the Swedes
might import; and this caused difficulties in the case of
margarine. The Swedes, however, were at all times most
co-operative and gave the program every consideration.
In addition to food, they were able to supply some shoes
and blankets.

Another duty of the Stockholm office was to see that
supplies were routed from Göteborg on Sweden's west
coast to Haparanda on Sweden's northeastern boundary.
Investigation had proved that supplies routed from
New York to Göteborg, picked up there by the Swedish
national railroads and carried to Haparanda, spent far
less time in transit—three weeks on the average—than
did supplies shipped direct to Finnish ports. This was

due to the fact that the Finnish railroad rolling stock was in bad shape and the supply of fuel scanty. Moreover, her ports were frequently frozen in winter, and there were not enough icebreakers to keep them open. Occasionally the Swedes had no freight cars available since they had already lent many of these to Poland. However, the Swedish railways usually were able to put cars at the disposal of the Quakers' forwarding agent in Göteborg so that shipments moved promptly whenever emergencies required.

The Swedish Civil Defense Organization was most helpful at this stage of the work. This government agency was originally created to house refugees and purchase supplies for them, and such activities had given it contacts with many sources of supply. The organization put at the Quakers' disposal an English-speaking executive, Herman Huldt, who kept Andrews fully advised with respect to supplies. Huldt also acted as interpreter with other members of his organization who had useful specialized information. Andrews' first step when he had an unexpected call for supplies was to present a request to Huldt, either orally or in writing. Then after Huldt and his colleagues had considered the character of the merchandise needed, they would secure bids from various merchants and recommend to Andrews the best supplier from the point of view of delivery and price.

If delivery of orders was held up, Huldt and his colleagues would put pressure on the supplier to meet the Quaker requirements. Sometimes it was necessary to consolidate shipments with the forwarding agent in Stockholm for shipment to Haparanda. At other times the suppliers shipped direct to Haparanda and Andrews advised the forwarder there that the consignment was coming. Duplicates of all this correspondence went to the field staff in Lapland, who kept in constant touch with Haparanda.

The Germans had destroyed most of Finland's warehousing facilities; this presented another difficulty. However, the supply lines were short, and the field staff maintained close relationship with customs officials and the forwarder at the Finnish border. Thus they could time their shipments so that the existing warehouse facilities in Lapland were not overloaded, and also ship their supplies exactly when they were needed. Additionally, the arrangement reduced the danger of pilfering. As for that, however, the honesty of the Finns, under constant temptation to increase their scanty rations of food and clothing, was inspiring. In one instance, for example, a bale in a shipment of clothing was broken open en route. When it reached its destination the clothing which had fallen out of the bale was all contained in a separate bag.

Other groups in Stockholm which rendered invaluable help to the Andrews office were the Swedish Red Cross, Radda Barnen, and the Co-operatives. Swedish merchants as individuals were greatly interested in doing everything they could to insure the success of the Committee's project. For example: The Danish sugar industry had only large sacks in which to ship its sugar. These awkward carriers made small-scale distribution in Lapland difficult. Andrews decided, therefore, that the sugar should be repackaged at the border in Haparanda in small containers. The Swedish merchant who sold them milk provided these and got them to Haparanda in time for repackaging the sugar.

The field staff could order by telephone or letter any supplies which had not been visualized when the program was planned. One day, Rovaniemi telephoned

Andrews to ask for a hospital barracks. Since the medical field was one in which the Quakers are not particularly experienced, he asked the Swedish agency whether or not it could include this in its program. It could not. However, although the original Quaker program did not provide for such an item, Andrews and the staff felt that there was a real need and kept on asking. As a result, the Civil Defense Organization secured the barracks for the Quakers within a period of three weeks.

This Stockholm office shared with the field staff the duty of rebudgeting the work as new funds became available. Since all expenditures abroad were being made in terms of Swedish or Danish kroner, and since the budget was dependent on prices obtained from merchants in these countries, it was necessary for the Stockholm office to keep in close touch with wants in the field, to translate them into terms of estimated expenditures, and whenever changes in policy were involved, to relay the information to Philadelphia.

Andrews returned to Philadelphia in May of 1946 and was succeeded by Lloyd Somers of Rochester, New York, a non-Quaker who had left his life insurance business to care for itself while he gave a year's service to Quaker work, with which he long has been in sympathy.

The Stockholm office under the management of Andrews and Somers had at the date of writing purchased and shipped $170,000 worth of Swedish and Danish foodstuffs and supplies for Finland and handled the shipping through Sweden of $360,000 worth of gifts in kind, clothing and shoes. Also, it has purchased and shipped from Sweden to Germany $200,000 worth of milk, soup, and medicinal supplies.

The Stockholm office serves also as a clearing center

for some other European Quaker projects. During my stay there, Joseph Howell of the Quaker staff in France was in Sweden for the purpose of purchasing a shipload of lumber to be used in building homes and barracks in Normandy. The tiny Stockholm Quaker office became his own, and the staff his assistants. Howell had paid the estimated shipping bill before he left for France, but a few days later the shipping agent notified Somers that the cost of transportation had been underestimated and that the balance due must be paid in Stockholm the following morning; otherwise there would be a delay in unloading the cargo. Somers learned of this through a telephone call transferred to him where he was having dinner with me at a Stockholm hotel. His conversation with the shipping agent and the way in which he conducted the business would have rejoiced the hearts of every contributor to the Service Committee's work. He was just and kind but firm, exceedingly firm. The ship was unloaded the following morning and on schedule.

Many hours every day are spent in finding supplies, purchasing them, obtaining shipping licenses (the Swedes are most generous in granting these licenses for anything the Quakers need), and arranging for the shipment of odds and ends of emergency supplies which the field staffs order. To date these varied and sizable activities have all gone forward in that tiny, unheated ten-by-fifteen-foot office. But all this will soon be changed, because the Quakers now have inherited the two rooms which UNRRA vacated when it closed shop in Stockholm. These are in the former German Embassy, conveniently located near the center of Stockholm's officialdom. This winter Somers, or his successor, will luxuriate in two furnished, heated offices.

Quaker School Feeding. Kemijarva

Quaker Conducted Orphanage, Tornio

Silent Grace, Quaker Work Camp, Autti

Personnel, Quaker Work Camp, Kittila

Children Playing at Hirvasvaara near Their Schoolhouse Which Was Destroyed by Enemy Planes

Children's Toys Displayed in a Store Window, Rovaniemi

Typical Finnish House (Note Fire Hazard Ladders)

Haying in Lapland

Rebuilding Great Railroad and Highway Bridge, Kemi

Highway Approach to Rovaniemi

Potters Working Their Clay

"Thank You, God, for Good Food"

Karelian Evacuee

Yard Broom in Foreground—House Broom at the Door

Children at Kemi—The Raised Hands Indicate Relatives in the United States

School Children Singing at Rovaniemi

Far North of the Arctic Circle, Finland

Similar Cemeteries with Soldier Dead Are in Every Community in Finland

Quaker Barracks and Day Nursery, Rovaniemi

Twins at Quaker Day Nursery

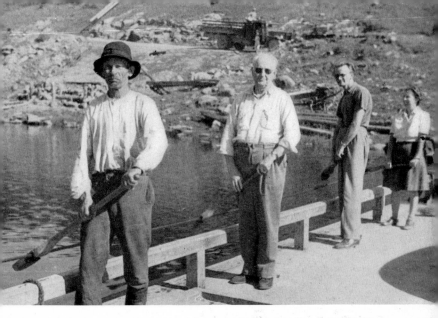

Passengers Helping Ferry in Finland

Charcoal Truck Generating More Gas

Ready-Cut Culverts at Forest Edge to Replace Those Which Were War-destroyed

Sawmill near Arctic Ocean

Quaker Work Camp Sewing Project, Kittila

Truck at Quaker Barracks, Rovaniemi, with Relief Supplies

Quaker Day Nursery at Kemijarva

Three Finnish Social Workers

A Typical Finnish Couple

All That Is Left of a Home—Man's Dearest Possession

Rovaniemi Rising from the Ashes Two Years After Having Been Eighty
seven Per Cent Destroyed

Reconstructed Midnight Sun Tourist Hotel in Rovaniemi

CHAPTER VII

Quaker Workers Reach Finland

FIVE REPRESENTATIVES of the American Friends Service Committee, only two of them Quakers, reached Rovaniemi before Christmas 1945. They were joined by a Stockholm Quaker, Lena Sundberg, wife of a distinguished Swedish educator.

The first arrival was "Bill" (J. William) Fredrickson, a member of the Swedish Covenant Church, who secured a leave of absence as instructor at North Park College, Chicago, to perform this service. Fredrickson, a tallish blond young man in his late twenties or early thirties, is a son of Swedish immigrants. He has friendly, smiling Scandinavian eyes and a rollicking sense of humor which expresses itself in contagious outbursts of laughter. Practical, direct, energetic, and businesslike, he also is gentle and kindly. There is about him, too, a suggestion of wistful idealism. His Swedish background makes him especially *en rapport* with the Finns. As a former leader of a Quaker work camp in the States Fredrickson had a good working knowledge of Quaker ways and methods and a great respect for them. He left his teaching job for the Lapland service. And he also left his fiancée in Chicago. She joined him, however, in the fall of 1946, and they were married in Rovaniemi, where they directed the relief program during the winter of 1946–47.

Plans for the wedding had been under way previous to my arrival in Rovaniemi in July 1946. As a step in this direction his fiancée had made application as a field worker to the Service Committee at Philadelphia. It in turn submitted the application to the field staff in Finland which replied by cable, "Unanimously Welcome Helen."

In late November of 1945, Fredrickson arrived in Rovaniemi ahead of his colleagues for the purpose of getting barracks built in which he and his fellow workers could live and have their working headquarters. This was absolutely necessary, because at that date only a few of that town's destroyed buildings had been replaced.

Thomas Harvey, leather manufacturer of Philadelphia, graduate of Haverford College, a Quaker, and a member of the AFSC board, had accepted assignment as director of the project and was the first of the group to join Fredrickson. Somewhat older than Fredrickson, Harvey, a redhead, outwardly dour though inwardly gentle and kind, was seemingly his direct antithesis. But their basic desire to serve mankind, plus Harvey's inward warmth and gentle humor made them particularly effective teammates. For belying his outward reserve Harvey had an effective way of breaking down barriers between man and man. Once after a few formal sparring preliminaries with an important foreign office official, Harvey bluntly asked, "What's your first name?" The official gave it, and Harvey said, "All right, from now on you are Charlie and I am Tom." This broke the ice jam and opened the way to a fine, harmonious relationship.

This same direct quality of Harvey's frequently puzzled the Finns in the early days of the work when some of the residents still questioned the Quakers' motives in coming to Lapland. Whenever word would reach Harvey that any of them had expressed fear that the Quakers were there to make converts he would see the spreaders of the report and say, "Sure, you are right. We are going to make good Quakers out of all these young Finns." Even though he was expressing the exact opposite of the Quaker purpose his seeming frankness served to dissipate the fear.

Along with his direct and brusque qualities Harvey has an almost boyish naïveté. Once he saw an Esso sign and hurried in to greet the men on the assumption that working for an American company they could speak English. Another time he hailed a lone Negro (a sailor) on the streets in Helsinki with the question, "Are you an American?" And when told, "Ah shore am," Harvey and the sailor laid the foundation for a fine friendship.

The four women members of the Finnish field staff reached Rovaniemi shortly after Harvey arrived. One of these was Nancy Foster; she, Harvey, and Lena Sundberg were the only Quakers in the group. Nancy Foster, an Ohio farm girl, was graduated from Swarthmore College about ten years ago. She had later become a dietitian and served in that capacity for three years as a representative of the Service Committee in Civilian Public Service Camps in the States. Also she had been stationed in the Committee's Philadelphia office for several months. Her Quaker background and her experience with the Service Committee, plus her qualifications as a dietitian, peculiarly qualified her to help in the Finland project. Along with these qualifications she had two other striking ones. The first was a sturdy farm-nurtured body which equipped her with seemingly inexhaustible reserves of energy. I have seen her start a busy day at seven in the morning, do innumerable things all day long until midnight, and show fatigue only when an occasional moment of repose revealed lines of weariness in her face. Of equal, perhaps even of greater importance, was her ability to remain patient and kind despite the pressure of her duties. These qualities, combined with a wholesome working philosophy, a sense of Quaker humor at its best (sly, quiet, and whimsical), and a ready, quick, good mind, made her a most agreeable companion as well as a highly competent staff worker. Regardless of the demands upon her, I never heard her complain, never caught a note of querulousness in her voice.

Another woman member of the staff who arrived in Rovaniemi in the fall of 1945 was Mary Barclay of Wichita, Kansas, granddaughter of A. A. Hyde of that city, the founder of the A. A. Hyde (Mentholatum) Manufacturing Company. Miss Barclay, a Presbyterian and a graduate of Middlebury College, had taken a year's course in the Haverford College Graduate School of Reconstruction and Relief Training. She also had served as a codirector in a Quaker work camp in the States. Her strength is that of the pioneer woman. Her open-faced, middle-western friendliness, combined with her cultural background, enabled her to gain quick and warm friendships with the Finns.

The third woman staff member was Naomi Jackson, an Episcopalian of Canada, niece of Canada's distinguished painter of that name, and a graduate of McGill University. Miss Jackson, herself a painter of note, had exceptional linguistic talent. She had taught German at Wheaton College (Massachusetts) and originally applied for service with the Quakers for the purpose of joining the staff they planned to send to Germany when the way opened. She agreed to take the Finland assignment when it was clear that the initiation of the work in Germany would be delayed. Outwardly Miss Jackson, slender and smallish, appears to have limited reserves of strength. Actually she is as tough and strong as whalebone, able to travel great distances daily and hold countless interviews.

The fourth woman member of the staff was madonna-faced Lena Sundberg, a Quaker of Stockholm, whose husband is head of a boarding school. Lena Sundberg's mature judgment, sensitive feeling, and warm, understanding heart became invaluable aids to her colleagues. Over and above her native talents, her knowledge of the Finnish language, people, and customs and her tender sympathy for the Finns in their need helped her fellow workers to avoid many potential difficulties.

This group, all its members experienced in Quaker relief or work camp projects, was joined in March 1946 by Herman Keiter, Lutheran professor of philosophy in Hartwick College, Oneonta, New York. Keiter, "a verray, parfit gentil knyght." He also had seen service in Quaker work camps in the States. Keiter is a devoutly religious man of middle age, whose sincerity is apparent in every line of his honest, kindly face. His quiet strength made him the natural choice for director of the Finland project after Harvey returned home in July 1946.

The Service Committee uses the utmost care in selecting its field staff for relief projects, both Quaker and non-Quaker. The all-important qualification each worker must possess is technical competence combined with a desire to help in meeting a human need with a sensitive spirit. The worker should possess, too, a "spiritual center" that is active in his life—something that keeps tenderness and understanding alive. Though he might possess every other quality, he would be unacceptable if the milk of human kindness in him had soured. He must also have tact, a co-operative attitude, and an ability to submerge political ideology, sectarianism, and national prejudices. This latter is important, since the submergence of beliefs in these fields enables the worker to move freely across all barriers of politics, religion, or race in the discharge of humanitarian service. Any man or woman, regardless of creed, color, or nationality, who possesses these qualities has the makings of a good relief worker, since they enable him to minister with friendliness and kindness to any human in need. This, the faith that beneath every exterior lies a person who is precious to God and worthy of dignity and respect, is the hard core of Quaker belief.

One of the women of the field staff in a report to the Philadelphia office added a "Note for the Personnel Office" which said: "I find the most important qualifications a relief worker must have are a knowledge of how to chop wood, haul water, fix carbide lamps, typewrite by candlelight, cook without recipes and with ingredients in containers with name and directions in language one doesn't know."

Naturally the Quakers occasionally make a poor selection, but in the choice of foreign service personnel these mistakes are kept to an almost irreducible minimum by a screening process which they conduct with characteristic caution. As previously indicated, a high percentage of workers on foreign service have had some previous experience either in their Quaker work camps or domestic relief projects. And finally, as is set forth in one of Bill Fredrickson's letters, which follows, the selected workers are given a short but intensive course of instruction in the nature and purpose of their new duties.

When I was in Rovaniemi the American staff was assisted by Sade Saarinen, a smallish Finn who is an ordained pastor of the Lutheran Church and an ex-sergeant of the national army, and Toben Lundsager, a tall, blond, serious-faced young Dane. Saarinen is the official interpreter, but Lundsager has exceptional linguistic abilities as well as an uncanny knack of finding anything or everything to do and of doing it well.

Fredrickson had his first assignment, that of erecting the barracks with material shipped from Sweden, well under way when Harvey arrived.

In the Quaker files I found copies of two letters which Fredrickson wrote friends in the States, the first dated November 21, 1945, the second February 13, 1946. Parts of them belong in this story because as well as showing his attitude toward the work they give graphic impressions of the conditions which the Quakers met and the problems they had to solve. "The days are getting longer now," one of them reported on February 6, 1946. "This afternoon about three o'clock when the electric lights went off suddenly according to their habit, we could still see our way around the room to find the candles."

In the first of his letters, Fredrickson wrote of the strangeness of his being in Finnish Lapland almost exactly on the Arctic Circle, when but a few weeks ago—it seemed almost overnight—definite word of the AFSC's selection had reached him in Chicago. On his arrival in

Philadelphia on September 4 to start his training program, he found that the committee had picked Finland
as his field of service and applied for a passport for him.
For four weeks after that, he worked like a horse. Of
this period he writes:

> . . . we had lectures and attended meetings which made us
> familiar with the functions and methods of the Service
> Committee, and which gave us a better understanding of
> the Society of Friends which we will represent. I must
> say that the deep admiration and respect and feeling of
> kinship with the Society of Friends and of the work done
> through the Service Committee has grown immensely with
> this closer contact. In addition we had conferences with
> returned foreign service delegates and also with Dr. Hertha
> Krause of Bryn Mawr College, probably the outstanding
> authority on international relief. In our spare time we pur-
> chased our equipment, and I had lessons in German con-
> versation every day. We were a jolly group of trainees
> bound for far corners of the world—Finland, France, Italy
> and China. . . .

He tells how, one Saturday afternoon, a staff member
of the Service Committee had asked him if he could be
ready to start on the following Wednesday. He was; and
on October 4, he sailed for Europe in a three-thousand-
ton freighter. Arriving in Stockholm, he met Steere and
Andrews, with whom he spent two weeks, helping to
work out innumerable details which had to be looked
after before he could leave for Finland. Among other
things he helped with the purchase of prefabricated
barracks in Sweden. He tells of his arrival in Rovaniemi
as follows:

> I can't adequately describe the feeling that came over
> me as we drove into this ghost city of Rovaniemi in the
> white arctic night in which one can see as if by moonlight—

shock, horror, disgust, wonder, sadness—perhaps a mixture of these. Everywhere on all sides were the heaps of rubbish and the ugly outlines of chimneys against the sky that once were homes. Half-houses that somehow remained standing, now house a family or two, and smoke coming out of the ground reveals where someone is living in a cellar. Only a few non-wood buildings escaped total destruction, but they were of course gutted by fire....

In his letter of February 1946 he told his friends that although he had been in Lapland three months he had not yet "frozen to death," and that while life there was certainly different from anything he had ever experienced it was not so different as one would expect. Snow, he said, was always with them but it was only two or three feet deep. The main roads were kept pretty well plowed. The winter to date, he reported, had been unusually mild, only a few days below twenty degrees. The arctic dark was a more unusual experience. At Christmastime, the sun didn't get above the horizon at all for several days, and at the end of February it did not rise until 9 A.M.

Fredrickson wrote further:

One of the most satisfying parts of this program has been our efforts to help schools get their kitchens into operation. For many reasons—lack of equipment, lack of a place to cook, or just inertia—many schools were not doing any feeding. Partly through our offer of supplementary supplies, our encouragement, and a supply of kettles, almost all now have kitchens of one sort or another in operation. They cook in all sorts of places from regular kitchens to bathhouses, but the children get the food and that makes us happy. We are trying to visit every school and to keep visiting them repeatedly. It's a big job, but very enjoyable. In addition to collecting information we talk to the children, tell them about America, sing to them, (often "Old MacDonald had a Farm" which they know in Finnish), listen to them sing, and sometimes have a cup of coffee with the teacher (usually ersatz)....

Last week, Dr. Sigfrid Sirenius, president of the Settlement Association, and one of the great spirits of Finland, was with us as we celebrated our "wedding feast"—co-operation with the Finnish Red Cross and the settlement association. He is the father of the settlement movement and really a great man, with the gentle dignity and kind simplicity that only the truly great have. Also with us was Aaro Tolsa, settlement pastor, who has built up the settlement program for the timber workers in Lapland and who in his 20 years in Lapland, has done many things to better the life of these workers.

In all that we do we are trying to carry out that vital element in the Quaker faith that every human being is uniquely precious in the sight of God. We intend that our help shall not be merely a distribution of material relief but something personal, an act of love. We hope to show these people here that there are people in America who care, who are concerned personally about them, and thus in some way to build a bridge of understanding and good will between our peoples—the only secure foundation on which to build in this tottering world....

One general impression I want to share with you, and that is the overwhelming consciousness one feels over here of the terrible conditions in Europe. Even in prosperous Sweden the awfulness, the suffering and tragedy that is Europe is in the very atmosphere. There is more news about it in the papers. One cannot escape it by laying the paper aside. Everywhere one hears or feels the question, "How can Europe survive the winter?" and "What is America going to do to help?" I hope that we will not fail to see the need and respond.

The job of organizing the child feeding and the work of clothing distribution was well under way when the first supplies reached Rovaniemi. By this time the barracks had been built and furnished with tables, stools, beds, mattresses, blankets, dishes, pans, buckets, lamps, and every other article of home and office equipment, purchased by Andrews in Stockholm.

As one of the first steps in arranging co-operation with the Finns, the staff typed out letters to teachers in each of the 268 schools in the province of Lapland. A sample follows:

Rovaniemi, Finland
December, 1945

Dear Miss ———:

The Americans of Finnish extraction have been collecting funds to make possible a program of supplementary child feeding in the schools of this area.

We the American Friends Service Committee staff in Rovaniemi and Kemijarva have been commissioned to help in this work and are happy to tell you in this letter that an initial shipment of pork, milk, and soup will be delivered to you in January. We are enclosing directions for preparation and amounts to be used weekly for each child.

We are pleased that you have a kitchen in operation and want to help you in any way possible. We plan to visit your school in January or February and look forward to meeting you then. We have already opened our office in Rovaniemi and would be glad to hear further from you.

Our best wishes for the coming year.

Very sincerely yours,
Thomas B. Harvey
American Friends Service Committee

A typical visit to a school began with an explanation to the teacher of the program, emphasizing that it is the financial support of the Finnish-Americans that has made it possible. The name of the teacher and the number of students were entered upon a card, together with details about any present feeding, the need of the school for kitchen equipment, how much food the children were bringing from home, and arrangements for delivering supplies.

The return visits to schools after the feeding had started were rich experiences for the workers. One of them in writing of such a visit said: "The children were a wonderful group, polite, shy; to see their smiling, happy faces and to learn from their teachers that they are getting their lessons better because of the food is a rich reward for our efforts."

A report from Rovaniemi dated December 12, 1945, describes and illuminates the experiences of the Quaker workers in their round of calls on the schools:

The significance of this feeding program in the schools stands out so clearly when you have done a little visiting! ... The appreciation of the teachers, who are among the real heroes of Finland today, is so great that it cannot be expressed in writing.... We are now making a point of talking to all the children in each school. It lengthens a visit but it seems to mean so much that Americans are here. When we ask how many have relatives in America about 10%–20% raise their hands.

After stopping briefly at 7 or 8 of the points on our route, we came to Raudanjoki, whose name has lain like a stone on my mind. *There are 42 school children in Raudanjoki who will have no school and no teacher until next September.* In January we had to pass them by with our food, since—having nothing else—they naturally have no school-kitchen either....

On this trip, however, Miss Jackson of the staff asked the young woman who cooked for the road workers if she would be willing to cook for the school children. She agreed, provided her employer approved. When the

Quaker worker secured the employer's consent, she wrote:

I can't describe how *happy* I feel about this case; I hope to visit them sometime and maybe take along some of our paints and musical instruments, and if possible a Rovala settlement worker and songbooks, so that we can make a real day of it with the boys and girls, who at present have too few outlets for their active young minds!

Tuesday and Wednesday we spend in the church village, chiefly at the school barracks where the 180 children have to attend in shifts from 8 A.M. to 7 P.M., due to great space shortage. They have insufficient benches and blackboards, no maps for geography lessons, no kitchen for cooking in. But persuasion and public pressure (plus the tempting thought of good AFSC food waiting for a chance to come in) have resulted in the construction of a special little cooking-hut, where an old army stove was being rigged up at the time of my visit (I got a nice photo of a bunch of boys and dogs in front of it). It will be a triumphant moment when that kitchen starts operating, which I hope it already has; the school principal told me that over 40% of the pupils come from outlying villages and board in private homes, where the pickings are very lean indeed. I gave what felt like *dozens* of talks in those two days: one to 75 in the "middle-school," entertaining them vastly by telling that I had always been the "bad one" in school, made to sit at the front middle desk right under the teacher's eye—and now here I was standing in the teacher's place and talking away to them! Then I gave more talks to the different classes of the public school and what is more—a whole set of art lessons, one in each class, a couple of days good hard work. They have no art teacher and when word got around that I'd done a bit of that I couldn't escape. I hope I put some dynamite (of the Quaker variety of course) into their timid efforts. . . .

Miss Jackson wrote of an occasion when she was asked to speak:

As I hadn't prepared anything to say I spoke straight from the heart. I started out in Finnish and got along for a long time (maybe two minutes). Whatever it was I said to these people we feel are our friends, and to whom we bring greetings from friends across the sea—messages in words and in more solid form of food and clothing—however I managed to get it out, it went right from my heart to theirs and I felt that the divergences of birthplace and time vanished under the impact of human kindness. It was a very good meeting and it continued in smaller groups out in the snow where their magnificent reindeer and pulkhas were tethered.

So, braving an arctic winter with the temperature sometimes at forty below zero, traveling by automobile, truck, reindeer sleds, or even skis, the Quaker workers from America visited the communities of northern Finland, got to know the people, their conditions of life, and their needs, and at the same time explained with words and their presence what they were planning to do. The Quakers have learned from long service that their friendly approach and interest serves measurably to submerge professionalism in relief work, to keep it on the level of help from friends to friends.

Close co-operation with the people to be helped was early initiated and constantly maintained. A paragraph from an early report tells of a meeting the Quaker staff held by candlelight with their local committee whose personnel included the head of Rovaniemi's rationing authority, the Finnish Red Cross, some settlement workers, a minister, the wife of a lumberman, a watchmaker, a carpenter, the business manager of the hospital, and representatives of other social and political groups in the town.

The distribution of clothing began on December 18, 1945, when a first consignment of forty-seven tons arrived. The Finnish Red Cross, which had earlier been engaged to handle this operation, arranged a schedule of preference. Those who had suffered most from the war and evacuation came first, large families second, evacuees to Finland third, evacuees to Sweden last. The allotments were set by the committee, which with volunteer helpers made up packages, each recipient collecting his package and giving a receipt.

One member of the staff described a clothing distribution scene in a cold barnlike barracks in Rovaniemi. To it had come all individuals who had been allotted a share in the shipment just arrived. The room overflowed with paper sacks filled with clothing, each containing the share of a single family whose name was on it. These allotments had been made by the committee, which considered each carefully before making a decision on the basis of comparative needs.

"The loyal women committee members," he wrote, "had been there working in the cold for four hours, giving the recipients their packages as they filed by. As we were looking on, an oldish woman, although obviously in need of more and better clothing than her package contained, grinned widely at us, threw her arms around Tom Harvey and said 'A thousand thanks to our American friends.'"

By the summer of 1946, the Quakers had received and distributed 334 tons of food and clothing to more than 23,000 children in tragic Lapland and clothing to many more thousands of adults. In addition they brought in and distributed 114 tons of seeds, tools, and miscellaneous articles.

None of this distribution was made impersonally or on a "mass basis." The Quaker workers shared the lives of their Finnish friends, demonstrating both their interest in them and human as well as humane concern for their welfare. It is small wonder, considering the staff's attitude, that in October 1946, before the workers left for the central Finland project, the people of Rovaniemi gave them a party.

All those in the town with whom they had been closely associated were present, from social workers to truck drivers. Nancy Foster wrote me:

It was hard, very hard to leave such good friends, but the wonderful things they said about what it had meant to them to have American friendship as well as American physical aid, we will never forget. They also spoke of the way in which working with the Quakers had enabled the group to cut across political and social boundaries ... the banker's wife and the leading Communist were both on our committee ... and how valuable that had been for the community. We were deeply touched by it all.

CHAPTER VIII

The Quaker Barracks in Rovaniemi

DURING the summer of 1946 a one-story barracks served as working and living headquarters in Finland as well as a symbol of the spirit and purpose of the staff. The doors to this building swung open on well-oiled hinges to every comer. It was evident to visitors that the staff was not on a slumming expedition. These primitive quarters lacked nearly every convenience for comfortable living; the members ate simple food which they cooked themselves; they worked long hours. These outward evidences of sincere, earnest devotion backed up by service and self-sacrifice give a convincing demonstration of the dynamic force generated by the complete union of physical work, creative thinking, and Christian consecration.

The staff lives almost literally in a glass house. Men, women, and children come and go in an almost continuous stream. Those in need are made especially welcome. While I was visiting them, a truck returning from some far-off place at 2 A.M. brought in a ten-year-old towheaded boy with serious eye trouble. The staff had no facilities for caring for this kind of case, but neither had anyone else in town. So, as always when in doubt, the inhabitants passed the problem to the Quakers, who put him to bed. No more was seen of the tired little fellow until the next noon when with tears of loneliness running down his cheeks he joined us for lunch. An ample meal soon made him feel better. Although we could not understand a word of each other's language, he and I became most companionable before two days later the staff sent him away to a hospital where they had made arrangements to receive him.

There also come to the Quaker barracks national and local government officials, other relief workers, doctors, nurses, teachers, writers, cameramen, and all field and camp workers. Here, emergency supplies are stored for quick delivery. Here, too, the members of the staff, live, eat, work, and have their being. They carry in every drop of the water they use and carry out all garbage. Their toilet facilities consist of a near-by outhouse. Their refrigerator is a cave which was formerly an air-raid shelter.

At first the staff occupied two buildings. But during the summer of 1946 they all crowded into one of them in order that the other could be used as a day nursery for the children of working mothers.

This barracks has a room about eight feet long by eighteen wide at each end with a passageway through its center. On each side of the passageway stands a three-decker bed furnished with thin mattresses spread over what purport to be wire springs. They are only slightly more comfortable than bare boards. The roughly carpentered frames sag, squeak, and wobble.

The small cubbyholes also contain two wooden closets divided into sections for storage of laundry and personal belongings, a wooden table, two stools, and a Finnish stove. Opposite one of the beds is a glory hole into which is stacked valises and trunks, bundles, blankets, and what have you. Above this, assorted odds and ends of clothing hang on nails. The foregoing describes the men's living quarters at their end of the barracks. The women's end is similar in most respects except that it is kept in much better order. Each member of the staff makes his own bed.

There are two Finnish stoves in the barracks. These are in reality brick structures reaching from the floor to the ceiling. Wood is put on the fire through iron doors standing about two feet above the floor. Each stove has three long flues. Through the first, smoke and heat flow from the fire to the ceiling; through the second, down to the floor; up another one to the chimney, through which what's left of the heat—and that is very little—escapes. Most of it serves the purpose of heating the bricks, which in turn warm the rooms on either side. Those long triple flues also slow down the draft and prevent the wood from burning too fast.

The small passageway between the outer and inner doors at each end of the barracks serves as a washroom. Its sole furniture is a wooden box on which rests a bucket of water, a wash basin, cups, and a mirror. Unless you are a sissy, you shave with cold water. If you are a sissy and if there is any warm water left in the teakettle on the cookstove, you may have some by going and getting it.

The emergency storeroom adjoins the men's room. It is piled high with crates and sacks of staple foods ready for quick dispatch to a newly enrolled school feeding unit, to work camps, or to orphanages.

The Service Committee's office in Lapland is also

the staff's living room, its kitchen, its dining room, and its reception room. One long table serves as the office desk. On it are typewriters, a telephone, and all records not filed in manila folders in a near-by wooden, sectional closet. On a similar table, the staff eats its meals. Sectional wooden closets hold dishes—few and of many styles—cutlery of varied patterns, kettles, and the like. When I visited the establishment, there were barely enough assorted dishes, cutlery, kettles, pans, and skillets to cook and serve a meal for all hands. Nancy Foster explained that the staff believed it better for them to have only enough for their bare needs, since that was all most Finnish families had. But all this changed shortly afterward when Roundy, a young, attractive Finnish volunteer came to help out. She felt that such niggardly furnishing was hardly respectable, went to the Red Cross on her own, and brought back adequate kitchen and table equipment.

A small, wood-burning cookstove standing on brick foundations and a one-burner electric plate furnish the heat for cooking. Big boxes in the corner and a wide board serve for dishwashing and for preparing food. A cot for overflow visitors stands in one corner, and backless wooden stools complete the furnishings. The floor is covered with a coated, thickish paper composition.

In this house the Quaker workers live with no more privacy than decency demands. Once a titled woman came for a visit, bringing a maid and fourteen pieces of luggage. Once two women came from a distant town, remained two hours "just to look at the Americans," and said hardly a word the whole time.

Another time the staff was asked to accommodate for two nights a social worker, because there was no other place to put him up. He liked the company and the food and stayed on and on, week after week. He left only after a woman of the staff put a tea towel in his hands and asked him to help dry the dishes. This was too much; so he disappeared for three days. He might still be there but for the fact that another worker was given his bunk when the staff doubled up so that they could free one barracks for use as a day nursery .

The staff observed one striking difference in manners: few male Finns or Swedes were trained by their mothers, as American boys are, to help with housework. Only a few men of either nationality offered to help either in cooking or in cleaning up after a meal. Some of them seemed to feel that such work was below their dignity. Others, however, would help after they had been covered with a tea towel, and soon began to think it fun. One evening when the women had gone for their *sauna* I washed the dishes and pots and pans alone. While I was at this job a Swede who was stopping there en route to a work camp came into the room and asked me to haul him to his camp the next day. He wanted to go in a comfortable car instead of the truck. Although I was cleaning up after him as well as the others, he left me to the work as soon as I granted his request.

The barracks seems to have the same attraction for drunks that honey does for flies. They are harmless but interested visitors and may come at any hour of the day or night. One evening at sundown—about 11 P.M.—the young women staff members at the dry nursery in the adjoining barracks and a few men work-campers were playing some kind of "ring-around-the-rosy" singing game. Their spirited, innocent fun attracted a drunk. He wandered into the enclosure, sat down on the steps, watched and listened, absorbed, without interfering in any way. A companion, also drunk, came and tried forcibly to lead him away. But our new-found friend refused to go because, as he said, "I like it here."

Anyone who comes over to the barracks at mealtime is invited to eat. Almost without exception all accept. It is impossible to guess accurately a half hour before mealtime how many will sit down at that crude table. Someone will telephone and ask to bring one or two people and then arrive late with four or five. A truck may drive up at any time with unexpected guests. None of this ever phases the staff. The fare is simple and plain —for breakfast hot cereal, coffee with powdered milk, and bread and butter; for luncheon a stew, potatoes, bread, butter, and coffee; for the evening meal a menu somewhat more varied. Most male and female visitors, except for the European men already referred to, offer to help peel potatoes, fetch wood and water, set the table, and wash dishes.

Previous to my leaving Stockholm for Rovaniemi I telephoned the staff to learn what they would like me to bring along. Nancy Foster answered, "Fresh fruit please. We miss that the most." When informed that the Stockholm stores had just received a consignment of apples from Chile, she gave an exclamation of delight and remarked, "We haven't seen an apple since we left home last fall."

My arrival at the barracks with a box and a suitcase full of fruit and marmalade created some excitement. But the fruit supply—except for lemons—did not last long because the staff, each keeping only one apple and one orange, shared it with their Finnish friends. Roundy gently rubbed and rubbed her apple, tenderly touched it to her face, enjoyed its fragrance, and then put it carefully away. When asked why she did not eat it, she

answered, "I'm taking it home to my young brother."
The lemons, used sparingly, lasted long, and there was
marmalade on the table for several meals.

In these circumstances and in this manner the staff
makes practical its working theory that only by sharing
completely in the way of life of the people whom they
are helping can they create real fellowship. The proof
of this pudding is the eating. In all the lands to which
they carry relief, the Quaker volunteers have a special
hold on the affections of the inhabitants. These adventurers in goodness receive only their food, their living
quarters, and a minute allowance—ten dollars monthly
—pocket money. Their real pay comes in the satisfaction
of work well done—that and the knowledge that the
coming generation will be stronger physically, more
kind and generous spiritually because the hands that
helped them have been delicate and friendly.

Utopian? Of course! Futile, because it does so little
in a world that needs so much more? No! The most use-
less thing in this distressed modern world is the conviction that because things are so bad individual action
cannot avail. The real hope for civilization rests in the
conviction of individuals that come what may, each one
of us will continue to grope through darkness toward
light.

So perhaps such individuals, expressing their faith
through their works, may in the end come together and
conquer the world by peaceful means to the end that
the highest form of life on our planet may settle its
differences by some means higher than those of the
army ant.

In such undertakings of the spirit a thousand years
are but a day—a watch in the night.

CHAPTER IX

A Work Camp Project

THE PURPOSE OF A WORK CAMP

QUAKER work camps are undertakings in which a number of young people, usually of both sexes, volunteer to perform during the summer months useful service in areas where there is social or economic tension. The institution dates from the depression of the nineteen-thirties. In 1946, approximately five hundred young people worked in such camps at home and abroad. It is a new technique in social service and has tremendous potentialities.

These projects involve many kinds of work. In all instances, however, the personnel of the camp performs manual labor. The workers live on or near the job, cook their own meals, and do for themselves generally. They associate at work and socially with the people whom they seek to help. In this and other ways they gain and give insight into social problems. Best of all, the experience commonly serves to broaden their spirit of understanding, tolerance, and friendship.

The Quakers have found from long and varied experience in the United States that the work camp has serious claims to being a superior way of relieving a community in that it avoids the dangers inherent in outright giving: weakening of morale or wounding of the spirit. This is accomplished in part by insistence that the people and the community contribute to the material project with their work and supervisory skills and, when able, with materials and tools.

The Quakers hold that people who do hard physical labor together for a common purpose find it easy to understand each other even though in their normal lives they may have been kept apart by the barriers of race or class; that common work makes friends; that it is hard to dislike a man with whom you have dug a ditch; that when you are nailing shingles to beat the weather or spading a sewer to outwit typhoid, there is little difference between a poor man and a rich man; that the distinctions between white, black, and brown men tend to blur if not fade when they toil together to achieve a common good.

These projects, as sponsored by the Service Committee, are designed to give young people an opportunity to serve for the purpose of demonstrating a belief in the brotherhood of man as well as the fatherhood of God. The projects are conducted with the conviction that methods of nonviolence alone can effectively remove the causes of conflict. The work demands sacrifice, but it offers an opportunity to serve in areas of social and economic tension.

In one of their booklets the Service Committee emphasizes that a number of American colleges allow credits for work in their camps and adds:

Where there is despair, where there is bitterness, where there is suffering caused by man's harshness to man, the American Friends Service Committee seeks to take material relief and a healing sense of human fellowship. It tries also to help young people to understand the causes of conflict and to prepare them to take their part in building a peace founded on justice, freedom and cooperation. Though the Committee's work is small in the face of the world's great need, it is a symbol of the desire of thousands of individuals to do something practical and personal to help those who suffer.

Which means that the work camps are concerned less with national reconstruction and relief than with moral and spiritual values. They are a tested, positive, and unique effort to build peace and to destroy the roots of war, a major hope of Quakers and many others who work toward lasting peace; and for the following reasons:

(a) The work camp seeks out conflicts from which international war stems, establishes itself in the midst of them, and in a variety of ways shows both the campers and the people for whom they are working how Christian truth might dissipate the differences and build justice and peace.

(b) The work camp is an adventure in true democracy. To this end, its personnel always includes sincere and able members of the so-called working class as well as of the so-called privileged class. This is done on the theory that although convictions may not always be changed, nevertheless persons of conflicting convictions, through living and working together, can come to a warm and human appreciation for the views of people with whom they disagree.

(c) A generation ago William James pointed out that war calls for the extremest and supremest in man, and emphasized that some moral equivalent must be found if international war is ever to be destroyed. The Quakers believe that through the exacting discipline of physical work and the demands of a Christian faith that dares to enter every area of life, the work camp at its best can supply much of this equivalent. The Service Committee has found that hard and often monotonous physical work, simple food, primitive living quarters, and lack of conveniences endured in the spirit of sacrifice serve effectively to drive the rule of the material from the hearts of men. Work campers have testified that two months in camp have proved as valuable for them as a full year or even more of college or university study.

WORK CAMPS IN FINLAND

During the summer of 1946, the Service Committee operated two work camps in Finland and co-operated in a third one. Seventy-seven young men and women, most of them between the ages of twenty and thirty, comprising nationals of six countries, manned these three camps and for one to three months gave their hard labor for the residents of three different communities in Lapland. They ate simple fare (for breakfast, bread, butter, hot cereal, potatoes, milk or coffee) prepared and served by a rotating crew of their own group, slept on cots in Finnish army tents, and were allowed only fourteen cents a week for out-of-pocket expenses such as stamps.

Finns and Americans served as codirectors of these Quaker work camps. Mary Barclay at Hirvasvaara and Bill Fredrickson at Autti had been members of such camps in the states. Each was familiar with the Quaker approach to the project and the spirit which guided it. Mary's colleague was Ingmar Rikberg, an able young Finn from Helsinki, who was a staff member in the

Rovaniemi barracks from the time the work started. Bill Fredrickson's colleague, Esko Saari, of Helsinki, was another able, fine-spirited, quick-minded social worker, who also had served earlier as a staff member at Rovaniemi barracks.

The steps for selecting the places for work camps and the nature of the service to be rendered were identical. Those taken at Hirvasvaara, as here described, will therefore serve for all of them.

The plan for the project was put before the central committee on rebuilding in Rovaniemi. The Quaker group at first proposed that they should help to rebuild the settlement building or give service in the homes of distressed people; but these ideas were discarded for practical reasons. Next, they proposed help in reconstructing houses destroyed or damaged in the war. This was approved. Officials of the commune were requested to select the areas for such service. They canvassed the field and designated the three districts which most needed help.

One of them was the Salla Commune, whose officials had their headquarters at Kursu. Quaker representatives went to Kursu to confer with these officials and found that the community in worst shape was Hirvasvaara.

Next, the Quakers met with members of the school board in Hirvasvaara. These people decided that a new school building for their one hundred children was their greatest need—the old one had been wholly destroyed. The Quakers reported this decision to the officials of the Salla Commune at Kursu, who stated that they had made no provision in their budget for the construction of a school building at Hirvasvaara during 1946. The Quakers therefore asked them to select some other kind of work, but emphasized that it must be in the field of greatest need.

Salla Commune and Hirvasvaara gave the same answer. The greatest need was homes for war widows with children, or for families in which the husbands were invalids. The Quakers agreed to this, and asked the officials to select the families. To give one illustration of this: When I visited Finland, the Quakers were building a house on ruins where lived a war widow with nine children. She was evacuated in both the winter war and later in the German war, during which the Finns drove out the Nazis. In the winter war she lost four cows and five sheep; in the German war four sheep, four cows, and ten pigs, her house, and all her household furnishings. The Finnish government had granted her 10,000 marks for rebuilding a home which normally would cost 25,000 marks. This from the government plus free Quaker work and free supplies such as nails—there are no surplus nails in all Finland—and homemade bricks, gave her a new house and a fresh start in life.

The way now was clear to take the next step, namely, to ask for a community meeting at Hirvasvaara to discuss the nature and purpose of the project. Quaker leaders explained at this meeting their methods of procedure, the steps taken to determine the work to be done, and the reasons behind the selection of families for whom they were to build homes. Finally they revealed who had picked out these particular families. After these points had been fully discussed and were clear and acceptable to all present, the Quakers asked the community to select an advisory committee to help them solve any problems that might arise.

Appointment of the advisory committee made the project official. The first move was to erect the campers' barracks, a one-story wooden building, approximately eighteen by thirty feet, with a small kitchen boarded off in one corner. It serves as a dining and living room as well as office. The rebuilding committee furnished the lumber and built the barracks. It also supplied the wood for simple furniture, such as tables and benches, and straw for the mattresses. The Finnish army lent tents for sleeping quarters.

The camp was now ready to function, and the Quakers asked for a meeting with the advisory committee. To the committee they explained that the Quakers always worked *with* rather than *for* a community. While they had most of the tools and equipment they needed and would supply everything else so far as possible, they said they hoped the community might be able to furnish a few things that they lacked. The Finns answered that they would do everything in their power.

One need of the workers was for a sauna, a Finnish bathhouse peculiar to that region. Two citizens of the town came forward to offer their own. One, miraculously intact, was assigned to the women. The other, much damaged, the Quakers repaired and assigned to the men. These bathhouses are almost as necessary to the inhabitants as bread and meat, for they are a cleanly people. For them, "a Saturday night without a sauna is almost no Saturday night." These small sauna outbuildings grace nearly every country homesite and all but the poorer sites in the towns.

A sauna has two rooms, one for dressing and one for bathing. The slatted flooring of the washroom carries off the waste. A great caldron filled with water stands in a corner. Under it, when a Finn prepares to bathe, a fire is built. Beside it lies a pile of stones which are heated at the same time. Large buckets or tubs filled with cold water stand about; and at one side are tiered benches where, after having soaped themselves, the bathers sit and perspire in an atmosphere filled with live steam generated by pouring water on the hot stones. When you can stand it no longer, a companion douses you with cold water; and so, at least once a week you are a new man.

The Finn regards his sauna with an emotion resembling reverence. One inhabitant told me that when he was a boy he once started to whistle a tune while having a sauna with his father, but stopped in the middle of a bar when his father admonished him that the sauna was a holy place. Here, he said, children were born, here men and women and children came to get clean inside and out and to cure themselves of many ills. To many it is a spiritual experience. The writer hereof offers no personal testimony as to this. But if cleanliness is next to godliness there may be something in the Finnish belief.

Once the saunas had been repaired, the communal rebuilding committee soon began to deliver lumber and other supplies, and construction work started. One crew dug trenches for the foundations of buildings, mixed and poured cement. Another, working at an inspiringly beautiful lakeside, albeit with primitive equipment, made bricks. Another hauled sawdust—the Finnish builder uses this filler between the false and true floor and between outer and inner walls for insulation against both cold and heat.

The personnel in the camp consists of twenty-seven volunteer workers, about evenly divided as to sex, and mostly between twenty and thirty years of age. The workers enroll for two months' service. When I visited the Hirvasvaara camp, its personnel consisted of seventeen Finns, four Danes, two Swedes, three Americans, and one Briton. One of the workers was Judy Hamilton, daughter of the U.S. Minister to Finland. At the Autti camp the roster by nationalities was nineteen Finns, four Danes, two Americans, and one Swede. The Kittila camp had ten Finns, eleven Danes, and six Swedes. The latter was under the direction of Erik Sundberg, the son of Stockholm Quakers.

The Finnish work campers were enlisted by Mary Barclay, Bill Fredrickson, and Herman Keiter on trips to Helsinki. The qualifications of all were screened, and each was recommended to the Quakers by the Christian Settlement Association or other social and welfare organizations; the Danish workers by the Danish Peace Friends, and the Swedes by I.A.C., an international work group with Swedish Quaker affiliations.

They are awakened each morning by the vigorous ringing of a cow bell and sit down to breakfast at 6:00. At 6:30 in the dining room, already cleaned of dishes, they reassemble for fifteen minutes of devotional service. The silence of the meeting is broken only by a brief scriptural reading. Anyone who attends one of these quiet gatherings for worship is sure to have a moving spiritual experience. They create a feeling of timelessness and universality—take one's thoughts completely away from the world of things as they seem into the vast realities of the spirit.

After the manner of Quakers everywhere, one of the camp leaders brings the meeting to an end by shaking hands with his neighbor. The group then rises to its feet, joins hands in a circle for a few seconds, and then, at 6:45, off to work they go in all directions. They return for lunch at 11:30, resume work at 12:30, quit at 4:30, and have supper at 5:30. The Quaker practice of offering silent grace precedes each meal.

The early morning period of silent worship was initiated at the suggestion of the Service Committee. Through long experience staff workers had found that it is easy for the camper to get so buried beneath the day-to-day duties and chores that he loses sight of real issues.

To remedy this [wrote the Committee] a brief period is set aside each morning directly following breakfast when the entire group assembles and sits together in silent meditation. This is the time to restore perspective, to recall the purpose of this particular day's task, to understand how it is related to God's deeper purpose in the world; to consider one's relations with fellow campers, with people in the community, with those who toil and struggle everywhere; to have raised in him the question of what he is on earth for, and to become inwardly aware, inwardly refreshed, inwardly strengthened.

In inaugurating this form of service, the leaders explained that it had been adopted in work camps in the United States because the workers belonged to many different religious groups, and silent worship conflicted with no other form of worship. Also, since it enabled each individual silently to follow his own creed's approach to the Deity, it had served to unite them. Again, it helped overcome the barrier of language. This method best helped give the group a oneness of spirit, purpose, and comradeship. A few weeks after the camp started, one girl remarked that at first the period of silence seemed terribly long but that now it seemed very short, for she had learned how to worship in silence, in her own way.

It should be said that difficulties arising from difference in language are not formidable, since most educated Europeans are bilingual. Moreover, the American staff members, immediately upon assignment to an area, begin to study the language of the country. In addition, Quaker ways, such as silent grace before meals and gentle and considerate presentation of problems, work to unite spirits and purposes as though there were no barriers of language. Also, each language group quickly learns some of the popular and national songs of the others; and their song fests generate much good fellowship.

But perhaps the most important influence in tearing down walls of habit and language is the Quaker approach to life. In nearly every European country where the Quakers work, their native associates carry into camp the habit of deference to superiors in rank. When the European workers at this camp took their turns at waiting on table—this job is rotated—they always served the leaders first. Pleasantly and tactfully, the leaders explained to them that in the Quaker concept of life there is no rank—that all are equal. Thereafter, it was first come, first served, in that camp.

Once a week, the whole camp holds an evening meeting at which the members discuss all plans and problems of their work, all rules and procedures for life in barracks. The Quakers hold that they should suppress nothing except impulses to suppress, that arbitrary power should never be created or enforced, that individual participation and acceptance of individual responsibility are the roots of social conscience. The workers also discuss camp disciplinary problems such as promptness in obeying the call to bed and to meals, of orderliness in the living quarters. In this manner everyone learns all he needs to know about the work and about community living. Every camp has one or more "problem" workers, most of whom sooner or later respond to the pervasive influences of persuasion.

No open charges are ever made against any individual, and thus no culprit is offended. Instead, the discussion of late rising and late meal attendance, for example, is opened by someone with the statement that everyone should try to be prompt. The reason for this is presented: the prompt arrival shows consideration for others by not interrupting silent grace, by lightening and simplifying the work of the housekeeping staff. At these meetings camp committees on work, recreation, and education also make their reports and announce the next rotation of work.

One minor problem is solved in the same way—that of keeping the camp headquarters in good order. In time, everyone almost instinctively picks things up off the floor and puts them in their places, straightens benches or tables or what have you, even if he was not responsible for the disorder.

The regular weekly business session which I attended devoted considerable discussion to the question of whether or not the campers should take a brief recess from building activities in order that they might help widows or invalid farmers with their haying. The procedure closely followed that of a Quaker business meeting. Mary Barclay told me later that this was not the case when the camp first started. Members who had previously worked in camps run by their governments, where strict discipline instead of democracy operated, at first were at a loss without the orders obeyed without question, the officer of the day who got people up in the morning, told off this worker or that to police the camp and put living quarters in order, and saw that everyone got to work on time.

Indeed, one group of nationals was at first openly critical of this Quaker proceeding, maintaining that there was too much talk and too little work. The Quaker leaders persuaded them to try this novel way for a few weeks. Within a month this group came over to the Quaker point of view. Later the workers most effectively made their little democracy function.

Once when the camp was selecting a leader for a special job, another problem arose. Two names were put in nomination immediately, and there were symptoms of a contest which might divide the camp. Mary Barclay and Naomi Jackson then explained how the Quakers handled such questions, whether they involved business or worship, emphasizing that it was also the democratic method. It was simple. Approach every problem with the query: What decision is best for the whole group and its work? They urged also that no individual try to force his ideas on the whole group, and they stressed the Quaker ideal of going forward in unity.

That set of ideas gradually took root. Consideration for others, while still not universal, resulted in greatly improved relations. Unity of thought and purpose and the good of the whole camp became the rule and not the exception. These adventurers in goodness have learned some valuable lessons—the democratic way of life for one thing; for another that subordinating personal ambitions and accepting the will of the majority makes the service of the group as a whole much more effective. And inevitably this makes for improved international understanding.

SOCIAL ACTIVITIES

The children of the Hirvasvaara community, who had lived through six years of war and its aftermath, were undernourished. This made them susceptible to illness and especially to skin diseases. Some of them, as a result of evacuation, had not been in school for four years.

These facts prompted the camp workers to request their Finnish advisory committee to appoint a subcommittee on child care. This was done, and at successive meetings the new committee worked out a plan for supplementary feeding and supervised play. Seventy children came the first day, and as there was not camp equipment enough to care for more than fifty-five at a time, they had to divide the applicants into two groups which came for feeding on alternate days.

Another consultation with the committee resulted in grouping the children by families. Children of four large families were to form the first group. As a result, sixty hungry little Finns appeared! Resolving this crisis involved a long trip to a telephone for the purpose of calling up Rovaniemi, nearly one hundred miles away, with an urgent request for more equipment. It came with all speed in the "package truck," a fearsome ton-and-a-half vehicle with the appearance of a Black Maria and the gait of a bucking bronco, which was constantly on the road hauling personnel and emergency supplies all over Lapland.

A journey in the package truck is a harrowing experience. Compared with it a jeep is a beauty-rest mattress. Theoretically it has springs—actually it has only what appear to be springs. A ride in this liver-shaker over the gravel-surfaced roads of Northern Finland furnishes the proof. People with false teeth or floating kidneys find it especially hazardous. But it can and does get over the roads with the speed, though not the grace, of a deer. At the Hirvasvaara camp, as always, it saved the situation by bringing so much equipment that the camp could feed all of the children daily.

During the first sessions the children stood far to one side, silent and watchful. Soon, however, under skillful, friendly guidance they began to play games and give each day's gathering the air of an outdoor picnic. When I was there the meal and the play session that followed were the main event in the lives of these innocent, war-tossed youngsters. On all but rainy days, which are few in Lapland in the summer, the food is cooked out of doors at the site of a war-destroyed house on the grounds of the former schoolhouse. The children sit at luncheon under pine trees, on logs, and some even on the charred foundation of the schoolhouse itself.

The camp workers decided that they should offer some diversion for the older as well as the younger children, and arranged with the local advisory committee to hold a party, with games and singing, on one night each week. More than one hundred youngsters came the first night, and at succeeding sessions the number was steadily augmented by adults.

The workers at the camp devote one evening each week to the study of Lapland, its people, products, climate, and other phases of its national life.

COMMUNITY WORSHIP

The camp workers informed their advisory committee that occasional visitors expected at camp would be able and willing to address church services, should the community wish it. Two of the Quaker workers, one American and one Finn, are ordained Lutheran pastors, and since this was an all-Lutheran community, with neither church building nor regular pastor, the proposal was eagerly approved. Church services have frequently been held under the open sky on a hillside adjoining the camp. One woman offered her home for the purpose, and the camp workers were able to provide a speaker for the following Sunday.

Occasionally citizens of the community arrange church services themselves, to be held in a home. Whenever this happens they extend a special invitation to the group at the work camp.

A lady once invited the work-camper staff to have coffee with her, both before and after services—the custom of the country. The hospitable Finns drink coffee, real or imitation, as habitually and ceremoniously as the English drink tea. When the workers arrived, they found that she had borrowed the necessary china from nearly every family in town. The war's destruction nearly stripped Finland of such refinements of life, and she has been too busy trying to build essentials to bother with replacing such trifles as cups, saucers, and table trimmings.

THE WORKERS AS SEEN THROUGH COMMUNITY EYES

One of the war widows for whom the Quakers are building a home visited headquarters at the end of a day's work to invite the workers to her home for coffee. Quite impulsively, she added, "I feel several years younger with you here. You must understand that when one who has fought alone for many years to keep life in several children suddenly finds so many friends, troubles which once seemed so very important and difficult grow light!"

Earlier, this same woman had told one of the camp workers that she had lain awake many long nights thinking how difficult must be the life of these campers, who had come from comfortable homes to this far-off wilderness just to help strangers.

"When this hard stretch is over," said another woman, "we hope you will come back sometime as our guests."

One man said to a camp worker, "I don't believe that one of these houses would have been built this summer without you." The building master and others have expressed the opinion that skilled workers could not have done better work than these unskilled volunteers. Invariably, the workers always are invited to wakes and all other communal gatherings.

During the two active stages of the war, many families of this district evacuated their children to Sweden. Constantly, mothers of these little exiles come to camp bringing letters from them and ask for a Swedish interpreter, for many of these young Finns, living in Swedish homes, attending Swedish schools, have with the linguistic fluidity of childhood forgotten their native tongue. The Swedish members of the working force translate the letters, and taking dictation from the mothers, answer them. Some of the workers have had the touching experience of being present when an evacuated child returned to his home. Such children are strangers in a strange land, unable at first even to understand what their own parents and brothers and sisters say to them. Adjustment requires several weeks, even months.

The reason why the Quakers came so far to work so hard at first puzzled many of the Finns. Some even suspected a deep, sinister American design for commercial or diplomatic advantage. Understanding Finnish authorities plus food, clothing, and the exemplary life of the workers have dissolved such suspicions into thin air.

In time the workers and their associates became a real part of the community life. Men with their own wagons and horses brought them firewood, women dropped into camp to bring the workers such gifts, rich in these circumstances, as a loaf of fresh bread, a pitcher of fresh milk, a piece of cheese. Because the Finns are a deeply religious people they came to understand that the motive which brought these strangers was a spiritual one, an inward compulsion to extend a friendly, helpful hand to a nation in need.

AN EVALUATION

As previously stated, the Quakers carry over many of their religious methods and practices into their relief activities.

One of the fixed procedures of a Quaker congregation —as other sects would call it—is at stated intervals to read in meeting a series of queries and then discuss them and summarize the answers.

Some typical queries are:

Do Friends keep to plainness of habit, speech and furniture?

Do Friends avoid encumbrances hindering their growth in truth and the service of it?

Are Friends in amity, one with the other? Do they avoid backbiting and raising or spreading evil reports of any? Is care taken to put a speedy end to all differences?

Other queries deal with such topics as the care of

poor, education of children, observance of true moderation in all things, testimony against war.

The purpose is not only to inquire into the state of the meeting but also to encourage each member to examine himself at regular intervals and determine whether or not he is living consistently with the principles of the Quaker faith.

As the season for outdoor work in Finland drew near its end, the Quaker staff prepared a set of queries, which they sent to each worker. The purpose was identical with that which has prompted the Quakers for three centuries to pose and to answer questions that search their souls.

This document follows:

What do you think of the work camp as an instrument for giving relief? Have the people helped really been in need, and has the work camp effectively filled such need? Have these purposes been fulfilled in your camp: that work camp relief help shall avoid pauperizing people, hurting their spirit? ...

Has the work camp been effective in reconstructing community morale and spirit? If so, how? Has any religious spirit in the camp helped in this way? the friendliness of campers? ...

How effective has the camp been in furthering understanding and friendship between persons of different nations? between persons of different classes (as university students, young workers, farmers, leftists and conservatives)?

Has the work camp helped you and other campers understand the nature and workings of the society of the community surrounding the camp in a much better way than could be had only from books or formal trips? If so, how? (If possible, give illustrative incidents.)

How effective has the camp been in destroying some of

the causes of international war? as in being in the midst of and seeing how positive love might dissolve one of the conflicts which then multiplied result in war? as in extending national loyalties to include all peoples of the world and beyond them to a God who is the father of all? as in providing a moral equivalent for war, a situation in peace as demanding as that in war which calls out the deepest and supremest loyalty of man?

Has the work camp been able to help the campers be less dependent upon and devoted to material things such as material comfort and material security? Of how much help in this regard has been the monotony or difficulty of the physical work? How much help the simple food? the primitive living quarters? the lack of conveniences? Any others? What do you think concerning the need for such a new Franciscanism?

Has the work camp been successful in demonstrating the significant relationship between physical work and creative mental and spiritual achievement? In what ways, if any?

Work project: Was it well selected? Was the work efficiently organized? Did the work squads usually arrive at work on time? Was there plenty of work for all throughout the day or was there considerable time when there was nothing to do? What suggestions do you have for improvement of the work project? Describe any work projects that you would recommend for consideration for camps next year. Do you think the work project was considered sufficiently important or too important or not important enough?

Community contacts: Do you think the camp succeeded in getting as close to the community as it should have? What items of camp program helped in this way? What more could be done to give camp and community a fellowship of spirit?

Religious aspects: Did you feel that the period of silent worship was valuable? How? What if anything might have improved its effectiveness? What is your reaction to the Sunday services with the community? Was sufficient time and emphasis given to mediation or worship by the individual when alone?

In what ways during the autumn and winter do you plan to continue work camp attitudes, techniques, and philosophy? (This is one of the most important of the questions. Answering it properly should involve a careful study of the highest values of work camp and reverent search for opportunities to realize them in out-of-camp life.)

What features of the camp have you felt are of particular value and should certainly be continued?

What features of the camp have you felt of doubtful value, to be improved or omitted in the future?

It is possible that long after the workers have gone to other stricken areas the people of Hirvasvaara, Autti, and Kittila in Lapland, far from the main roads of civilization, will remember the integrity and the friendly impartiality of their friends in the work camp, a group which asked nothing of them but an opportunity to help them bear their cross in their time of tragic need.

An indication of how the people of Hirvasvaara felt toward the work campers was given in a note from Mary Barclay written in September 1946, after the camp had closed:

People from the village began to arrive to say goodbye at 5:30 the morning we left. Breakfast was eaten outside in an awful rush and then bags and people were loaded onto the truck. "Hyvastys" had to be said all around with many tears on both sides and finally the people sang hymns as the truck pulled out. The first truck took only Finnish campers so that they might catch the train to Helsinki. Stade went with the group to buy their tickets and to help them get off. He reported later that they had held silent meeting on the truck.

Those of us who were left behind spent the day washing up equipment, counting everything and packing it in big crates for the Red Cross. Women and children from the community were with us all day. Many brought yellow berries as a parting present. The second truck arrived about 1:00 and a little after 2:00 the last members of the staff said goodbye to Hirvasvaara. The children ran down to the gate alongside the truck and waved goodbye as long as we were in sight.

Those last few days were a very moving experience for us all, and one which we shall never forget.

CHAPTER X

Finland's Bare Shelves

THE BARE shelves and show windows of the stores in every Finnish town tell graphically and poignantly of the need for goods, and these can come only through foreign help. All commodities are strictly rationed. Clothing and shoes are almost nonexistent. One woman, a bank clerk, told me she had received only one shoe coupon in five years.

Show windows display crude wooden toys and a limited array of food supplies. Few of the commodities which we consider necessary to life, and which we can buy in almost any store, are to be seen. The Finns had no tea for five years, and even now only a scanty supply trickles in. One of Finland's most distinguished social workers, a saint in any man's language, joined us for tea at the Quaker barracks in Rovaniemi. Ignoring his tea, he began hungrily to eat the slice of lemon on the saucer. He told us that this was almost his first lemon, his favorite fruit, in five years. Since then a box of lemons and tea has gone from Stockholm to his home near Helsinki. For five years the Finns drank a tea substitute made from raspberry and lingon leaves.

The first real coffee for five years reached the Finns in 1946. It was fifth or sixth grade in quality. The allotment to each person was one quarter of a kilo, about one half a pound, which cost seven hundred marks, approximately five dollars in American money. During the war the base of their substitute coffee was barley and peas. Sugar is still rationed, one-half kilo monthly to each individual at a cost of fifty-three marks a kilo. A smoker gets one quarter of a kilo of sugar and the rest of this ration in tobacco. Each nonlaborer (manual laborers receive larger allotments) gets eight kilos of bread monthly, one kilo white, the rest black. Eggs cost about thirty to thirty-five marks (twenty-five cents) each; potatoes seven marks a kilo; tomatoes four hundred marks a kilo. Potatoes and tomatoes are rationed. Enough sausage for one meal costs approximately twenty-five cents, and a full monthly ration of meat is only enough for three or four good meals. Milk also is rationed. Adults receive one glass a day, a child three glasses—when obtainable. Milk is rarely to be had in Lapland. At times it sells for as high as four hundred marks a kilo, an almost prohibitive price. The individual butter allowance is one-half kilo a month; this costs 140 marks.

The Finns eat two meals daily. They have some ersatz coffee and black bread about 8 A.M., then their first actual meal, a combination of breakfast and lunch, comes at noon, and supper at five. Neither meal is comparable to the average American equivalent in variety, amount, or quality.

Packages from Sweden and of late from Finns resident in the United States bring them some coffee, tea, sugar, fats (usually Spry), and candy. Strangely (or is it?) some children under five years of age do not like candy, have to be trained to eat it. Some clothing and shoes also come through this channel. No one who has not seen conditions in Finland as of the summer of 1946 can appreciate how greatly the people need both clothing and shoes. I saw one young woman, a fellow passenger on an airplane, wearing as a light topcoat what unquestionably had once been the blue dressing gown of some American woman. At almost every turn one sees made-over clothing of this type. The need for shoes is tragic. An assistant cabinet minister, for example, was wearing shoes so badly worn and patched that they would be thrown away in America by almost anyone, no matter how slender his means. A report from a Quaker worker in Finland late in 1945 stated:

The other day the Home Care sister [a kind of a social worker] dropped in . . . and we had an interview. I won't report the details of the interview, but her shoes are worth talking about. In her work she must visit all parts of the commune—many miles from the road—and must often walk many kilometers. She had only a pair of low shoes, and these of thin leather, the soles almost worn through and starting to come away from the uppers.

A few weeks later a report to the Philadelphia office told how the staff had been invited on Christmas Day to have "coffee" at several different homes in Rovaniemi. It added: "At the first home, that of one of the well-to-do men in the town, we were greeted by the daughter in her stocking feet and when we went to leave, one of the sons volunteered to go along to show us the way, but had to wait till his mother took her shoes off and gave them to him, before he could go outside."

Nowadays one sees few gold rings in a country where

it is the universal practice for both husband and wife to wear plain wedding bands. The Finns gave the government their gold rings early in the war and replaced them with steel ones.

The Finns lack and greatly need additional foodstuffs, clothing, shoes, and tools. The limited area of good farmland, their lack of necessary horsepower for farming, their scanty textile production, and their almost negligible amount of foreign exchange with which to buy these articles or even simple tools for rebuilding combine to make their recovery slow and difficult.

Bad as is the situation visualized by their bare shelves it is not much worse than that which exists in the field of housing. The files of the rental boards in the cities are jammed with some 30,000 petitions for living quarters which wait, and wait vainly, for official O.K. About 200,000 permits for evacuees in the rural countryside are piled up behind the same dam. Ten thousand ex-servicemen have petitioned for building permits in the environs of Helsinki alone, but only six hundred could be approved. Lack of building material has created a vicious circle which cannot now be broken.

First, Finland has virtually no cement. It cannot be manufactured because there is no coal for this purpose. All stores of coal in the country are reserved for (a) merchant ships and icebreakers, (b) certain metal industries, (c) gas plants, (d) certain power plants, (e) heavy railroad locomotives. What little coal is left for cement manufacture is hardly worth mentioning.

Lack of fuel cripples the brick and tile industry also. The peacetime need was 150,000,000 bricks. During the war years production fell to 100,000,000. The present annual need is for 200,000,000 bricks, but only 65,000,-000 can be supplied.

Finland has large clay deposits, but here again lack of fuel makes it impossible to use this raw material. These clay deposits are also threatened by the land acquisition law, which would dispossess manufacturing companies in favor of ex-servicemen. If and when this happens, the brick factories will lose vital sources of raw material.

Even though the fuel crisis could be overcome, new difficulties would lie ahead. Transportation is now extremely limited. The number of motor vehicles on the roads has fallen by 70 per cent. The rest might do the job in a pinch, but there are no spare tires. Rubber imports are enough to cover only the essential repairs. Transportation of bricks is therefore prohibitively expensive.

Solve these problems, and Finland would still find herself in a quandary because—paradoxically—there is a shortage of lumber. This exists because most Finnish timber products must be shipped to the U.S.S.R. as reparations, and as much as possible of the remainder must be marketed abroad. Timber products are Finland's main item of export, the only goods with which she can pay for the imports of fuel and raw materials necessary for the industries working to satisfy the reparations which Russia exacts.

More than ever, Finland must warm herself with wood during her long, arctic winters. So most of the wood left over after Russia's exactions are satisfied must become mere fuel. In fact, the wood refining industries have had to surrender some of their choicest stores of raw material to the domestic stove.

The most perplexing problem of all, however, is felling the timber. This is mainly a question of man power. The normal consumption of wood for fuel is about 75,000,000 cubic meters, but currently only one third of this amount is obtainable. Lack of appropriate footwear and other equipment makes it difficult to lure workers to the lumber camps. So the shortage of shoes and clothing becomes a major economic problem for Finland.

Worse still, even though some kind of solution could be reached in respect to lumber, bricks, and cement, the vicious circle would not be broken because there are virtually no nails. The annual consumption of nails formerly amounted to between twelve and fifteen thousand tons. The need now, with thousands of houses, factories, and business buildings destroyed or damaged, is beyond exact calculation. In the summer of 1946 between eight and ten thousand tons were needed for current construction, but there were only 3,800 tons on hand. The situation is such that it is necessary even in the construction of boxes to see that there is a place for every nail. This extreme economy slows up deliveries to building sites.

The Finn is a natural-born builder. Leaders in the Quaker work camps never tire of describing the resourcefulness, industry, and all-round technical skill of their Finnish colleagues. One of them said, "Give a young Finn an ax, a saw, a hammer, and some nails, and he will build you a good house in a few days." Life in his barren country has made him that kind of workman. But he needs three essential materials for building purposes: lumber, bricks, and nails. Today all three are missing or scarce. Despite his desire and determination to build new homes and to make new goods for them his hands are tied.

CHAPTER XI

Finland's Own Relief Program

FINLAND's greatest social problem is that of providing new homes and creating economic opportunities for her population which was evacuated from the territory ceded to Russia. All but 30,000 of the 450,000 evacuees are Karelians; the remainder were residents of the ceded areas in the Salla Commune of Lapland and Petsamo.

Her second greatest problem is that of caring for disabled soldiers, war widows, and war orphans. She has nearly 50,000 crippled veterans as a result of two wars; men with amputated hands and arms, feet, or both, brain and spinal injuries, blindness, and other diseases, mainly tuberculous. She has 27,000 war widows and nearly 50,000 war orphans. Add other and smaller categories of war victims, and about 650,000 persons—one in every six inhabitants of Finland—are dependent on relief.

State aid is limited to pensions for her crippled soldiers and the families of dead soldiers and to indemnity payments to Finnish citizens whose property was ceded or destroyed.

Payments on reparations, which will require over 10 per cent of the Finnish national income for the next six years, make it difficult for her to care for her people until Russia's demands have been met in full.

War losses in lives, bodies, homes, industries, and other property, plus reparations payments, make Finland's load almost too heavy to bear. In his report on the present state of Europe, Herbert Hoover described her condition as the second worst in the world—Poland alone was in greater need. In a news release issued just before his departure for the Orient, he said:

... Finland has a fine determination to help itself. The Finnish people are working to their utmost capacity.

The removal of the 400,000 people from the area transferred to Russia amounts to about twelve per cent of the whole population being resettled among the remaining 3,400,000, of whom 400,000 in the devastated areas of Finland are in distress. This is a burden on a people already short of housing from destruction, and upon farms already small. It is a situation comparable to moving all of the people in the three Pacific Coast States onto the people East of the Rockies.

If the Finns are to be re-established to their place in the world, they must be helped and quickly.

But just as no one who visited Finland in 1946 can doubt the seriousness of her social and economic problems, no one can overlook the energy, ability, resourcefulness, and determination with which the Finns are tackling their problems. Everyone capable of work is on the job through long hours of every day. The government has strained its credit in its effort to meet social and financial obligations. Over and above that, the Finns, through private charity and with the aid of semi-official and voluntary relief organizations, are expending huge sums, for so small a country, in private relief. And they do this without duplication of responsibility and effort, without any waste.

The over-all organization, Suomen Huolto—Finland Relief—I have mentioned already. It was established in 1941 for the purpose of centralizing voluntary relief work. Twenty-four private associations engaged in this task, together with several governmental ministries which give it a semiofficial status, constitute its membership. The Ministry of Social Affairs appoints the chairman, the vice-chairman, and one additional member of its board. The Ministry of Defense selects one member of the board. Finland Relief deposits its funds in the state treasury. Its accounts are audited regularly and officially. So far, its costs for fund-raising and publicity have amounted to only 3 per cent of the amount raised.

Its field organization, based on the same principles as that of the upper administration, has a local relief center in every district with which the different welfare organizations are affiliated. The provincial relief centers act as bridges between the central administrative office and its field organizations, of which the chairmen are the respective provincial governors.

The activities of Finland Relief embrace all voluntary relief work for the benefit of war victims. In so far as the different classes of persons needing relief are represented by their own organizations, they get support, in the form of both money and goods, direct from Finland Relief, Inc.

Its welfare work consists, for the most part, in the usual donations of money and clothing and other so-called temporary relief. It has encouraged personal efforts to make ends meet, promoted cultivation of food crops, and stimulated 4-H club activity. Initial support includes the distribution of large money grants to war widows, invalids, and orphans, helping people of this class to procure professional training, furnishing tools and building supplies, meeting unforeseen emergencies.

When in 1944 Finland withdrew from the war, the government reinforced the status of Suomen Huolto in foreign relations by establishing a special foreign aid commission. The organization was now complete; the Finns had a semiofficial relief organization which channeled and generally supervised all domestic and foreign relief work, organized the transfer of relief funds and supplies, and at the same time permitted its member organizations the fullest possible freedom in their efforts to maintain relations with sister organizations abroad. Best of all, it avoided the establishment of a narrow, government-dictated system. The Finns carry out this program, vast for so small a people, with proper consideration for true democratic principles.

Finland Relief and its affiliated organizations have received substantial support from abroad. Sweden has been the principal contributor; in the fall of 1946 the value of its gifts was rising to 215,000,000 Swedish crowns, about $55,000,000. Denmark and Switzerland have given some aid, as well as America—not only through the Quakers but through the Salvation Army, the American Lutheran Church, and the American Red Cross.

Yet Finland is still in great need of humanitarian aid, a need which will continue to be felt so long as the country has to pay war indemnity to the U.S.S.R. Meanwhile she is reducing two big debts: one to her mighty eastern neighbor and the other to her own citizens. By now native aid alone has helped tens of thousands to get back on their feet and become active workers for the common good. Finland wants to prove herself worthy of aid by her record. During the past four years, her people have through private contributions raised 520,000,000 marks. That, when translated into American money at the present exchange rate, equals $4,000,000. But reckoned on a per capita basis it would equal $140,000,000 for the people of the United States. Reckoned on the basis of the comparative wealth of the two countries, the sum would be several times greater. Even that is not a fair comparison.

The United States has suffered no destruction of homes and property, has not ceded an area in which nearly 10 per cent of its population lived, has not been forced to pay heavy reparations to a victor. Over and above that, Finland's only important natural resources are farmlands and forests. I need not emphasize in detail the comparison in this respect with the United States.

However, Finland possesses one resource which is in these days of toil and privation her chiefest hope. Beyond almost any other nation, she has that quality of the unconquerable spirit which impels mankind to go upward and forward. No false belief that society owes them a living exists in the minds of the Finns. Individually and collectively, they ask only for the opportunity to earn a living. The only help they want is that which will enable them to help themselves. According to their prime minister, "We must show that we are worthy of outside aid to the whole extent of our need." This they have done with moving sacrifice and splendid courage. Even so, they welcome aid from abroad. Social Minister Eino Kilpi, in March 1946, expressed the feelings and the thinking of his Finns when he said, "Our thankful thoughts turn to the Quakers, to those who have personally braved the rigors of Arctic winter in flimsy barracks in order to help the needy. . . . The friendly assistance given us not only alleviates suffering but it bolsters our morale in grappling with difficulties of reconstruction and encourages us to rest our faith on the triumph of goodness in human affairs."

Neutral foreign observers have remarked that Finland seemed immune to the injurious effects of the postwar mentality, that slump into an alarming state of confusion and controversy which troubles so many other European countries ravaged by the war.

I did not hear a single Finn complain about the burdens which payment of Russian reparations has loaded on his people. They appear to accept this burden as an inevitable consequence of the war's outcome. Their first great concern is to meet these payments, promptly on schedule.

They have another concern of equal importance: to prevent the collapse of their human resources while bending every energy, using every resource, to meet Finland's material commitments through export. To date they have done this, but as an old Finnish proverb runs, "While the grass is growing, the cow dies." But their fierce love of their country, their unwavering pride in it, give them an almost superhuman determination to make it survive. All they want from the people of nations in happier circumstances is a little help toward survival.

Clothing for the ill clad, shoes for almost everyone, food for undernourished orphans, widows, and old people, artificial limbs for crippled ex-servicemen, shoemaker's tools, sewing machines, medical supplies for hosts of diseased men, women, and children, even nails, glass, hinges, and putty for building—all must come from abroad, either as relief contributions or as purchases with foreign currency. And the rebuilding of her shattered resources for production demands all of Finland's foreign currency.

Layettes for newborn infants are especially needed, together with oils and ointments. Finland's layettes today are made of paper, she has no oils or ointments for little bodies. She has few medical supplies for older children. Disease always follows war. When it kills older people, the loss is grievous but bearable. But an intact and healthy rising generation is the essence of the kind of national greatness to which Finland aspires.

FINLAND'S EVACUEE PROBLEM

The catastrophe which befell Finnish Lapland was tragic. Even so, the inhabitants of that area have one consolation: their homeland still belongs to them. Although they face almost insuperable difficulties of reconstruction, they have an opportunity to build their future on the ruins of the past. Their passionate love of home soil enables them to endure all hardships; their methodical, deliberate habits of mind and action enable them to plan soundly and well—to do first things first. And their amazing patience, which stems in part from their unending struggle with nature for mere existence, prevents their becoming restive because of slow progress. None of these qualities makes the life of Lapland Finns easy, but together they do furnish a foundation for a new life in the old home. With a little food, tangible expressions of friendship, and a small amount of other help, these Finns of Lapland—all but about twenty thousand are now back at home—will carry their burdens and work out their destiny.

But Finland has another and far greater problem: the Karelian evacuees, who on September 1, 1945, numbered 420,789 human beings. The Karelian situation is less dramatic than the smaller one in Lapland. It was not created by the sudden, wholesale, deliberate destruction of mine and fire but by the slow, steady, and incidental forces of war, which robbed the inhabitants of their houses and household goods, their factories and tools, their livestock and farm implements, and finally their homeland itself. It is difficult to rebuild the shattered lives of a people without homes.

Moreover, the distress of the Karelians has lasted far longer than that of the Laplander Finns. These innocent victims of war—nearly half a million in number—first lost their property and their land during the winter war of 1939–40. The reconquest of Karelia by Finland enabled a substantial portion of them to return to their ancestral land and begin life anew among the ashes. The fruits of their efforts and their hopes alike were destroyed again in 1944, when once more they fled to central Finland before invading armies. Their tragic quandary, now six and a half years old, is no longer news. But it remains Finland's greatest problem since comparatively few of these evacuees have found new and permanent homes.

These 420,789 Karelian men, women, and children are scattered all over the country. Such of them as used to live in industrial centers and other populous communities have tried to settle in corresponding localities offering the best opportunities for the practice of their skills. About 25,000 of them are living impermanently in Helsinki, and proportionate thousands in other cities.

Jyväskylä, with a 12,000 prewar population, has 7,000 Karelian refugees within its borders; the near-by Laukaa Commune with 10,500 residents is furnishing shelter for 2,300 ; Suolhti's 3,700 people are housing 800, and Aanekoski's 4,500 are caring for 1,000. These figures on prewar and postwar populations, the latter increased by evacuees, help to explain Finland's difficulty in her housing crisis.

Habitations have been built in many places. In Jyväskylä, for example, ready-cut houses supplied by Sweden furnish homes on a beautiful hillside at the edge of town for one thousand—about one seventh—of her Karelians. These houses are divided into four rooms, each with its own entrance, and each sheltering an entire family in each room.

To prevent impossible crowding into favored districts, the government has been forced to distribute these refugees arbitrarily. So tens of thousands of townspeople have been living on farms or in small villages; and this must continue until that troublesome lack of building materials has been supplied. In the autumn of 1946, many houses begun in the spring were still only half finished and uninhabitable. The government has met this emergency by commandeering one room in every home containing three rooms or more, and establishing evacuees in it.

The majority of the evacuees, however, are of rural origin, and about half, or something over 200,000 of them, are independent farmers and their families. By condemnation proceedings the government is appropriating and paying for land carved out from large farms for the purpose of giving homes and means of subsistence to evacuees of this class. But because of lack of farm implements, household goods, livestock, and building materials this will take time.

The evacuees have tried to be self-supporting. The majority have managed to find breadwinning jobs. A large number, however, must still depend on state relief. Out in the country, there have not been enough suitable jobs to go around. This condition weighs most heavily on townspeople. Even persons used to farm work have not been without their difficulties, inasmuch as agriculture in Finland is primarily based on small farms employing very little outside help except during harvesttime. Lumbering has offered the best opportunities for evacuee labor. Also, the authorities have leased lands for temporary cultivation by farmer evacuees. The fields allotted to them are quite small, on the average only between five and seven acres, excluding pasture lands. But the crops harvested from them, both human food and animal fodder, will in any case make things easier this winter than last for these homeless people.

Good intentions and energetic efforts notwithstanding, the evacuee population as a whole has not succeeded in making ends meet without outside assistance. Through the agency of special relief officials, established in every district accommodating them, state relief funds have been distributed to evacuees in need. Last winter the maximum sum paid out daily to adults was twenty marks, and fifteen to children. The cost of living having steadily risen, this dole was raised at the beginning of last June to twenty-five and twenty marks respectively. Even these sums are trifling compared with the cost of living. Although the state budget is already under a terrific strain, the dole will evidently have to be raised in the near future.

On the last day of October 1945, relief money was

paid out to 66,145 evacuees. During the winter the number of persons dependent on relief increased considerably. It grew to 83,835 persons at the end of January 1945, and to 84,511 at the end of February. The number dropped to 50,234 by the end of August, which brought the summer harvest season. The relief lists again grew in the early winter of 1946–47, although they were not expected to reach the heights of the previous winter. Among the 50,234 evacuees receiving relief money at the end of August, 19,832 were children under fifteen years of age, and 14,128 men and women over sixty years of age. The number of persons on relief, who on the basis of age ought to be qualified for labor, is thus quite small. Only 2,916 men between the ages of fifteen and sixty received relief money. This fact proves that the evacuees had tried to become self-supporting.

Caring for the evacuee population has naturally burdened the state with large expenses. The dole alone has involved hundreds of millions of marks during the current year. Also the government has had to spend much money to store salvaged property and to return it to the owners. Transporting evacuees and their belongings from place to place has caused more expense. Last spring, for instance, tens of thousands of them had to be conveyed to districts where it would be possible for them to lease lands for planting.

Relief measures for their benefit involve, moreover, the upkeep of a substantial official organization which costs the state large sums. The current budget listed expenses on their behalf at 850,000,000 marks. In the autumn of 1946 that original estimate had been exceeded by a hundred million marks and there was every reason to believe that the final figure will top a billion.

Besides this their need is in many respects of such an order that the state is not in a position to relieve it directly. The appalling shortage of clothing, household goods, and furniture prevailing among these unfortunate victims of the war is a case in point. When they fled from their old homes, a large proportion of them lost all their worldly possessions except the clothes on their backs. Purchase of new clothing and household goods is largely out of the question, because such commodities do not exist in Finland. Lack of cash side by side with prohibitive prices often complicates the problem of the evacuees. The state gives compensation for property lost in the war, but the process is slow, and only small sums have so far been paid. Even if the market were swollen with goods, many of the refugees would still lack the means to buy.

In short, the painful problem of the Karelian evacuees has not yet been solved. A large part of them are still dependent on state measures in the form of compensation for lost property and the transfer to them of arable lands as compensation for farms left behind in ceded territory. These measures are provided for by special legislation, but their realization requires time. In 1946, for example, relatively few evacuee farmers got new lands. Most of these people have had to live through the past winter under temporary arrangements, often in conditions of extreme crowding and material need, lacking in the primary necessities of civilized existence, largely dependent on state relief for even this meager subsistence. To complicate the problem, the Karelian evacuees include a large number of war invalids, war widows, and war orphans, who have a twofold burden of misfortune to carry.

Much of the first foreign aid, for understandable rea-

sons, went to devastated northern Finland. The Karelians have received relief from their more fortunate
countrymen and from Sweden, but they deserve help at
least equal to that given the inhabitants of Lapland,
who, despite their many hardships, are nevertheless
appreciably better off than the homeless, forlorn, often
forgotten but grimly struggling Karelians.

CHAPTER XII

Relief First: After Relief What?

As of the fall of 1946, there is every evidence that Finland will be in acute need for outside food, clothing, and medical relief aid for at least one more year, perhaps even two years.

Inadequate diet, insufficient clothing, and indescribably bad living conditions have been seedbeds for diseases which greatly handicap her people's ability to improve their lot more quickly.

Supplemental foods containing fats and vitamins not present in available Finland foodstuffs must be provided by non-Finnish charity if today's generation is to be able to produce a strong generation for tomorrow.

Clothing of all kinds and in large amounts is needed to enable the Finns to carry on their reconstruction work during the long, cold winters.

The Finns will need medicines in addition to food and clothing; otherwise they will be unable to check the spread of diseases which thrive on bodies poorly fed, clothed, and housed.

The American Friends Service Committee, with a

capable and trained staff which has a sound working knowledge of needs and conditions in Finland, gained from a year's experience, estimates that to enable this valiant country to continue her own rehabilitation it could effectively expend $500,000 there during the coming twelve months. As war costs go, this sum is a pittance, but carefully administered, it would save many thousands of lives for useful service, would enable thousands of Finns struggling against great odds to get a fresh start in life.

That is the immediate need in Finland. That is the great opportunity for the generous everywhere. Yet indispensable as are food, clothing, and medicine for a hungry, half-naked, half-sick people, these things are of the moment. American charity, while providing them during periods of acute need, should look beyond and try to find ways to encourage self-reliance and initiative and to create opportunity. And the philanthropically minded must work out a formula which gives an answer to the important question: After relief, what?

Finland, with her large evacuee population, furnishes the Quakers or some other group every element necessary for working toward the solution of the displaced persons problem, one of all Europe's most pressing and tragic. It can be solved by constructive action. But constructive action requires a program, money, and tools.

As I have already shown, during the summer of 1946 the Quakers demonstrated through three work camps in the province of Lapland that considerable impetus could be given the rebuilding of Finnish communities through volunteer work performed in collaboration with public officials. Because Finland had few small tools or nails, little hardware for doors or glass for windows, and no available bricks, the Quakers supplied such things and helped in the construction of a number of homes which otherwise could not have been built at the time. They did this without adding a greater burden to Finland's already overstrained foreign exchange. But of even greater importance, the presence in different communities of these helpful, friendly volunteers served to raise the morale of the struggling Finns.

Similar building projects of more extensive nature should be planned for the summer of 1947 in other parts of Finland. Such a program could be carried out without great cost.

Securing several hundred competent volunteer workers for three months of service is not a part of the problem. If funds were found, the needed workers could be recruited in Denmark, Sweden, and Finland. However, Americans also should share in this work. It offers a great opportunity for scores of young American men and women of college age. No other method would so well avail to teach them the conditions and the ways of a foreign land—a course in practical international relations—to say nothing of the lifelong satisfaction coming from helpful service to distressed people.

A program of this magnitude would first have to be discussed with Finnish government officials and approved by them. And they should select the communities, provide the lumber and other available domestic building materials, approve plans, grant permits, and designate the families for which houses are to be built.

That plan, though laying the foundation of recovery, is still primarily one of present relief. But satisfaction of another consuming want lays hold on the future. Finland has stark need for a few craft-study schools at which young Finns, male and female, could receive training enabling them to become useful, skilled citizens. Finland's large population of war and evacuee orphans and her rising rate of juvenile delinquency make some such measure imperative.

I visited a craft school which points the way—Kannaksen Ammattikoulukat, situated not far from Helsinki. The plant of this institution, formerly located in Karelia, had been destroyed in the war. The new school had been built, under the guidance and with the help of two or three men, by fifty as fine-looking fourteen- to sixteen-year-old boys as anyone has ever seen. The government gave them a ninety-seven-acre farm on which fifty sons of veterans and of evacuees are beginning courses of two or three years in agriculture, blacksmithing, and carpentry. This fall the number will be increased to seventy.

Private and state funds support this school. The cost per year, per student—they raise much of their own food —is about 30,000 marks or $200. The headmaster told us that they had lost everything but their courage, and that with this they were building anew in the hope that all of the boys would become good, useful Finnish citizens.

Generous Americans, with the help of volunteer workers, could help Finland build a number of such schools for boys and girls. In doing so, they would establish institutions that would make valuable and enduring contributions to Finland's social and economic life. Once built, these schools would require no further outside support; the Finnish government would take over at that point. Over the years they would give orphans and other needy, worthy young men and women the kind of training that would enable them to become self-supporting, self-respecting, useful citizens. Twenty such institutions in twenty years, would bring hope and opportunity to ten thousand or more young people, transform them from charges of the state to supporters of the state. And the schools would long stand as symbols of international friendship, which in God's good time will banish war from the earth. Work camp volunteers could be secured to construct the buildings if a few thousand dollars were available for the purchase of hardware and other supplies and equipment which Finland does not possess.

Another possible and important field of constructive help to Finland by foreign aid is the initiation and operation of small industries. This activity offers tremendous possibilities.

The Quakers, who seek only to serve their fellow men, never mix money-making with relief service. But they could properly employ an expert in the field of home industries to make a survey and draw up a program of homework requiring a minimum expenditure.

Once the program was perfected and the initial raw materials bought, the workers enlisted with help from the Finnish government and the enterprise launched, the Quakers could withdraw from the undertaking. The Finnish government, or perhaps still better the well-managed Finnish Handicraft organization, could take over from this point—find markets for the finished products, purchase and import necessary raw materials, and sell them at cost to the workers. The operation of such an undertaking would create many problems, such as source of raw materials, foreign exchange to pay for them, and search for markets. Each such, however, could be solved with a reasonable amount of imagination, initiative, and persistence.

The expenditure of $100,000 for purchase and distribution of raw materials and necessary tools and guidance in the making of useful, needed articles should create profitable employment for from five to ten thousand Finns who now are not only unemployed but also are a charge to the state. The profits from their work, if they were heads of families, could in one year's time, lift from the shoulders of the state the burden of providing for 25,000 or more men, women, and children on the relief rolls. The sale of their products would help to solve Finland's problem of foreign exchange, and finally, the example of people who had built their lives into those of their new communities would greatly improve the morale of all her displaced people.

What projects of this nature might be inaugurated? From a great variety of possibilities I suggest a few here by way of illustration.

Purchase and distribution of outfits for repairing shoes. The two the Quakers brought to the Kittila camp cost less than fifty dollars each in Denmark. Such a kit, with a working supply of leather and other necessary supplies, could be given to an individual in each community to become his property without charge after he had repaired one hundred pairs of shoes free for the people in his community. This plan worked perfectly in Kittila. Finland's worn-out shoes are greatly in need of repair. A hundred such kits would help myriads of them to last longer and at the same time would enable a hundred Finns to become self-supporting. This is a one-time investment. Out of his profits, the owner could purchase additional leather as he needed it.

Another project which could furnish profitable employment at a small initial cost for an even larger number of Finnish women would be to give them yarn and needles with which to make sweaters, mittens, and gloves. The women of Bohus, Sweden, now hand-knit woolen sweaters of such attractive designs that they have a ready sale at high prices in the United States. The Swedish Home Industries organization has agreed to provide Finland with instructors in sweater making and to give other help necessary in the early stages of such an enterprise, should it be started.

A few thousand dollars would purchase the yarn and needles with which one thousand women could make their first sweaters. Out of receipts from this initial lot, they could purchase yarn for more sweaters, gloves, or rugs. The Finnish women make beautiful woven rugs and knitted sweaters.

Other possible projects requiring small investments include pottery and china making. Finland badly needs both commodities. Small portable blacksmith shops would be invaluable aids in repairing old and broken-down machinery. Tailor's equipment is needed to repair clothes or to make them over. Sewing machines would be of great help.

Obviously, a survey by an expert in this field may demonstrate that some of the suggested activities would be impractical or difficult to establish. Obviously also, such an expert would be certain to uncover or suggest homework projects which are not now visualized. Such programs, if they are well conceived and ably operated, unfold and grow.

Carefully and broadly organized and competently directed, enterprises like these would in time provide income-producing work for countless thousands of Finland's unemployed or misplaced workers. They would, at the same time, help fill Finland's bare shelves, make her worn-out equipment last longer, increase her balance of foreign exchange—in short help effectively to accelerate the rehabilitation of her strained economy;

and they would bring fresh purpose and hope to all of the people of war-wasted Finland.

The all-important point is that generous American people at no great cost could help discover a working formula for Europe's pressing problem of the evacuated peoples. Such an undertaking has tremendous potentialities and implications.

One possible source for a portion of the funds needed for such a comprehensive and constructive program is the United States Government. Finland has made sixty-two payments to it on the $9,000,000 bill for supplies which her government purchased at the end of World War I. Her total payments of principal and interest to date amount to approximately $7,500,000. Since little Finland is the one nation in the world which has willingly and promptly met her World War I obligations to our government, it would seem most fitting and proper for us now to make available for her for rehabilitation purpose the entire sum she has paid on the old debt.

Such a generous and gracious act would do more than to help a just and friendly people through a terrible crises; it would impress the people of the entire world with the fact that American idealism, generosity, and spirit of friendly helpfulness held precedence over dollars. Just as the return to China for educational purposes of our share of the Boxer indemnity money created a spirit of imperishable Chinese friendship for us, so would similar action on making available for Finland's rehabilitation the amount she has paid on her indebtedness. It could create a basis for trust and friendship in a part of the world where both are so greatly needed today. In any case, it would give a tremendous lift to the efforts, purpose, and determination of a brave and noble people, the Finns.

Even though our officials should catch the vision and so act, the sum in question would not be sufficient to help the people of Finland through their crises. American philanthropy also would still have to help. But with such a start it would be possible to see the end of the road of Finland's immediate problems.

Besides speeding the recovery of Finland, such an undertaking would stand as a convincing demonstration to the world that America is trying, sincerely and sympathetically, to help all needy people everywhere; and that she does it for no purpose other than to help create the universal good society, which can grow only in the rich soil of friendship. It might even give them that partial answer to the riddle of life which Faust so long sought and found just in time.

Goethe described Faust as having made a compact with the Devil in which Faust agreed to give over his soul through all eternity in return for a single mortal experience so great and so satisfying that he could not but cry out, "Oh, stay; thou art so fair!"

The Devil then began with the aid of sorcery to give Faust one experience after another: great political power, military genius and success, as well as the most beautiful and purest of women. Yet all these and other gifts of the Devil left Faust cold. Finally in old age, after trying every heralded human triumph, Faust gave up the whirl of the great world. He commenced to devote his whole genius to reclaiming land from the sea, helping people build homes, raise their food, marry and bring children into the world, and otherwise to live happy, useful lives where, before he began, nothing could grow and no one could live.

In this setting with the voices of happy children and singing birds in his ears, with peace about him which comes in such surroundings, Faust, now at the end of his life, experienced the moment of perfect satisfaction. He voiced his great desire as he sank back to die: "Oh, stay; thou art so fair!"

Finland today offers the generous-hearted people of the world an opportunity to short-cut Faust's life and reach directly his finest moment.

Appendix

Finland's area is about that of the six New England states. Always it has belonged to the Scandinavian and western orbit of civilization. The earliest Roman and Greek writers who mention the "Finni"—particularly Tacitus— speak of them in connection with other peoples and tribes of northwestern Europe. The Christian faith in its occidental form was brought some eight hundred years ago to Finland via Sweden and partly through Anglo-Saxon missionaries. The first man to preach the Gospel to the Finns was an Englishman, Bishop Henry. During the Catholic time he was the patron saint of Finland. Likewise, the first to lead the Finns in an international enterprise was Bishop Thomas, a Scotsman and probably an Anglo-Saxon. He, with the co-operation of men from the other northern countries, organized and led a crusade against the east. In the sixteenth century Finland, like the other Scandinavian countries, became Protestant. This action connected her still more closely with the northern and western world.

During some seven hundred years, Finland was in union with Sweden, not as a colony or subjugated province but as an integral part of the Swedish-Finnish realm. Thus Finland shared the destinies of Sweden in war and peace; but over and above that, political and social institutions and public life in general followed the same democratic lines as did those in the rest of Scandinavia. From this experience the Finns gained a general outlook and a culture similar to that in other northern countries, although Finland, because of soil and climatic conditions and location, always was poorer than its western neighbors and lived under harder conditions.

Its close connection with Sweden did not mean the loss of the nation's specific Finnish character. The Finns always remained Finns, with their own habits and civilization.

In 1809 Czar Alexander of Russia conquered Finland and tore it away from Sweden. Even then, Finland did not become an ordinary Russian province. Her position was that of an autonomous grand duchy; she had her own administration, parliament, and laws, her own money, and even her own foreign public debts, which, as always, Finland paid. In the later part of the Russian period the czarist government tried to destroy the particular status of Finland, to deprive her of her national rights, and to make Russians out of the inhabitants. These efforts made no headway. The entire Finnish nation established and maintained a stubborn resistance against them, with no shrinking from sacrifices or from persecution by the czarist officials.

In 1937, after twenty years of independence, her 300,000 farmers, through increase of productive land areas and by better farming methods, were able to provide the nation with more than four fifths of its food needs. The production of wheat, for example, jumped from 6,178 tons in 1917 to 208,611 in 1937; that of hogs nearly doubled; butter production trebled, and eggs and cheese more than quadrupled. In similar percentages other farm products responded to the new purpose and the industry of the Finns.

It is in forest products, however, that the Finns really

shine. These are their "golden crop." Between 1917 and
1937 inclusive, the value of the output of all the wood-
working industries jumped from 1,398,000,000 marks to
9,095,000,000 (the normal exchange rate of the mark is
approximately twenty to the dollar, today it is 136). The
value of the output of all other Finnish industries climbed
from 3,585,000,000 to 11,981,000,000 marks.

During this same period the Finns increased railroad
and highway facilities by one third or more and multiplied
their telephone lines by more than ten; letters and parcels
carried by the mails doubled, as did newspaper circulation.
Classes in elementary schools grew from 4,664 to 14,908,
and the pupil population grew from 199,016 to 407,881.
Enrollment in secondary schools nearly doubled, as did attendance at both agricultural and industrial schools. Membership in athletic and gymnastic clubs and the number of
athletic grounds each quintupled. The number of doctors
in government and municipal employ was doubled, and
dentists quadrupled, while hospital beds were increased two
and one-half times.

At the same time bank deposits grew amazingly, co-
operative societies increased in number and membership,
home ownership doubled and more than doubled again;
motor busses in operation increased fifteen times, passenger
cars thirteen times, and trucks twenty times.

According to Finnish government reports, the Nazi
Storm Troopers, as they were pushed farther and farther
north by attacking Finnish soldiers in 1944, destroyed a
total of 16,515 buildings; 38,527 cattle, sheep, and pigs;
736 highway and railroad bridges; 2300 culverts, all fishing
equipment, telephone and telegraph lines, and much railroad rolling stock and roadbed.

The Germans destroyed not only buildings but most of
the tools in the Lapland province. Finnish losses included
550 mowing machines, 300 horse rakes, 160 threshing ma-

chines, 1,900 plows, 7,000 harrows, 1,500 scythes, 7,700 axes, 6,500 saws, 4,300 spades, and articles like grain drills, sewing machines, separators, etc., in proportion.

The Finns evacuated 47,000 residents of Lapland into their central provinces. About 40,000 additional residents of Lapland who were not in the direct line of Nazi destruction remained either in their own homes or in near-by forests until the terror had passed on.

It is extremely doubtful if Finland, especially the Lapland province, could have survived without the help of Sweden, which in every form was given with magnificent generosity. The ramplike bridge which connects Tornio, Finland, and Haparanda, Sweden, became truly a bridge of life during the fall and winter of 1944. Over it, ahead of Nazi destruction, fled thousands of Finns. At one time more than two thousand per day poured across it into the peaceful, secure haven of friendly Sweden. Few of them had adequate clothing; many babies were wrapped only in newspapers, countless people walked barefooted, carrying their all on their backs or driving their cattle before them. But in they came without red tape, hindrance, or delay.

The Swedes fed and clothed these moneyless, hungry hordes, gave them shelter, and in as many as four or five special trains daily, hurried all 55,000 of them on to central and southern Sweden, there to place them in homes, hospitals, and other institutions—and all of this without charge.

In addition to taking care of the evacuees during this fall and winter of 1944 for varying periods, the Swedes provided homes and every care for more than 100,000 Finnish children. At the present time 25,000 Finnish children are still living in Sweden either at the cost of the Swedish people or their government. On top of all of this Sweden has sent countless tons of free food, clothing, and equipment to Finland; numerous Swedish towns have adopted Finnish towns and sent food packages, clothing, sewing machines, and innumerable other commodities necessary to the restoration of normal living.

The death toll of Finland's soldiers in both wars was staggering—82,000 men, a number equal to 2 per cent of her total population. Comparable American war losses would have been three million whereas the total of dead and missing in all branches of United States military forces was 306,379.

The annual charge on her economy in caring for crippled soldiers, war widows, and orphans is tremendous. In addition she must find new homes and new ways of living for 450,000 of her people who were evacuated from the territory ceded to Russia.

These burdens, combined with the next six years' indemnity payment, which alone requires more than 10 per cent of her national income, call for almost superhuman effort. Only one third of this bill for "reparations" can be paid in wood products, which in prewar constituted about 80 per cent of Finland's exports. One third must be paid in machines and tools, the manufacture of which keeps Finland's factories operating at capacity. Most of the remainder will be paid in ships.

In addition, Finland must rebuild her war-destroyed areas, replace her war-destroyed equipment and her badly depreciated industrial machinery and at the same time, if she is to continue to exist as a nation, she must conserve and strengthen her most precious asset, the bodies and the spirit of her valiant men, women, and children.